Withnail and I
AND
How to Get Ahead in Advertising

Withnail and I
AND
How to Get Ahead in Advertising

Bruce Robinson

BLOOMSBURY

First published 1989
Copyright © 1989 by Bruce Robinson

Bloomsbury Publishing Ltd,
2 Soho Square, London W I V 5DE

British Library Cataloguing in Publication Data

Robinson, Bruce
    Withnail & I and How to Get Ahead in Advertising
    I. British cinema films – Scripts
    I. Title   II. Robinson, Bruce
    791.43'72

ISBN 0 7475 0359 1

The author's royalties will
go to the Save the Children Fund.

Photoset by Rowland Phototypesetting Ltd
Bury St Edmunds, Suffolk
Printed in Great Britain by
Richard Clay Ltd, Bungay, Suffolk

For Andrew Birkin

Contents

Introduction

Some weeks ago I was in Australia trying to be on holiday.
Cappuccino-coloured butterflies and asthma amongst the
sandcastles. I was on a Pacific beach with friends attempting to
join in with the breathing. I was also trying to get a handle on
this introduction. I should have known better. Aim at two
targets with one arrow and you end up missing both. I was
exhausted with post-production of *Advertising* and needed this
holiday badly. Directing a film is easier than writing one but
physically it wipes you out. Cutting a film is like doing
press-ups. Each one equal to a minute's screen-time. The first
five are easy. Seven and eight are getting difficult. By ten your
muscles disintegrate. We cut twenty-four minutes from our
first assembly of *How to Get Ahead in Advertising* and the
anxiety nearly killed me.

Asthma struck in the middle of the night outside a little
tin-roofed town called Macksville. A dash to the rusting
hospital where they shoved me on a device to measure my air
intake. The average breather hits around four hundred. I was
coming up forty-eight. Apparently a prospective corpse can
produce about twenty-five with the fucking death-rattle.
Oxygen on and in go the needles, the latter featuring pure
pharmaceutical adrenalin. Suddenly one's heart is converted
into a small diesel engine that could get a motorbike up a street
at about fifty.

'I'm told you smoke?'

'Like a joss-stick, Doctor.' (Get this attack over so I can
have another.)

Am I insane? I'm getting too old for illness. I'm clearly too
old for cigarettes. Cigarettes should be reserved for children

and it should be illegal to sell them to anyone over sixteen. I am also too old to worry about writing introductions. Two days behind an oxygen mask convinced me the link I was seeking between *Withnail and I* and *Advertising* didn't exist. And rather than murder myself trying to create one I decided to introduce these screenplays separately. The first, *Withnail and I*, is in many respects autobiographical. So for anyone who is interested, here are a few bits and pieces of my life.

When I was ten I failed the eleven-plus, and children suddenly became colours. Green for the brainy. Blue for the partially brained. And grey for the half-wits. Those who got the green and blue blazers went to the Grammar and Technical School respectively; because it was they, apparently, who could answer questions like:

> If a man fills a bath with water, and
> eight gallons are coming in a minute:
> (A) How full will the bath be after
> four and three-quarter minutes? And
> (B) If the water is rising at two and
> a half inches a minute, how high will
> it be when the bastard gets into it?

Like most greys I have never been able to assist with enquiries like this. They may as well have asked me what the idiot had for lunch. The Charles Dickens Secondary Modern School was built of yellow brick circa 1953. In its foyer was a plaster bust of the great Writer, and up his nostril a piece of chewing gum. This was my first introduction to Dickens. The Headmaster's name was Warren, a.k.a. 'Bunny'. I recall little about him except he hated children and had the kind of beard you expect a pair of testicles to swing from. Occasionally Bunny would freak and start bashing the inmates for no apparent reason. Sometimes he used keys to swipe a disliked head. On one occasion he actually came off his podium and went thug while conducting the Lord's Prayer.

But I enjoyed the Charles Dickens School, and especially on

my second exposure to Dickens. Because we were considered cerebrally inelegant they didn't try and shaft us dead with maths. What they did do was let us be in school plays. I got the part of Herbert Pocket in *Great Expectations*, and suddenly the rest of my life was mapped.

I was going to be an actor.

In those days (long before Mrs Thatcher's 'Economic Miracle' had paved our streets with gold) you could get a government grant. You could also get somewhere to live. I auditioned for the Central School of Speech and Drama and was lucky. I left three years later in 1967. By 1969 my career had taken an unfortunate detour into the nearest Department of Health and Social Security and I was on the dole. But I'd made a lot of friends at Central School. And I'd also started to write. Mainly poems on a derelict Olivetti in the bathroom. The bathroom was where I slept. We all lived in a large terraced house in Camden Town. It wasn't a very attractive area then. At night the Irish would get their teeth bashed out and knock on the door for glue. We called these itinerants Wankers and did our best to avoid them. If a Wanker got hold of you with a gut full of beer you knew you were in trouble. Everyone who lived in this house was male, ex-Central, and called a Skin which was a Liverpool term meaning friend.

This was the Skin's Hotel. It was owned by David Dundas (who would later compose music for both these films) and who made the Christian but serious error of allowing the less solvent amongst us to occasionally share his roof. So many moved in David was eventually forced to move out. Civilisation went with him and officials were soon on the step. We acquired a wing mirror from a motorcycle and bolted it to the first-floor balcony to deal with them. Anyone with a bald head didn't get in.

Some of the sweetest and some of the most terrible days of my life were spent in this house. Up all night smoking dope and listening to Dylan. 'Visions of Johanna', out on your back in beautiful ruins. I remember laughter so bad you had to crawl out of the room to escape.

Thank you my ancient Skins.

It couldn't go on, of course. The deficits were closing in. A constant stream of heads were outside shouting up at our mirror and demanding money with menace. We didn't have any money. Almost all of our National Assistance went on booze. Conditions continued to deteriorate until only two of us were left and the only stimulant guaranteed was frustration.

'Why can't I get a job?'

In the winter when it was too cold to hack upstairs I used to type in the kitchen with the oven on and its door open.

'Why can't I get a fucking job?'

'Shut up, will you. I'm trying to write and you're giving me the heeb. Things could be a lot worse.'

'Could they? You have an extraordinarily vivid imagination.'

'We could be a pair of Wankers.'

'Wankers? What's wrong with being a Wanker? Wankers know where they stand. All they gotta do is hod bricks and squat Sunday for some bone-idle employee of the Pope.'

'You wouldn't fancy it.'

'Wouldn't I? I fucking-well would. Down the church. Down the pub. Arse-holed as quickly as possible. A fight if you're a young one. Start singing if you're an old one. And a good spew outside the Odeon about three o'clock for both. What's the matter with that? The Wankers have got it made. They've got fridges and televisions and phones.'

If we had funds we'd sometimes tread it down to Delancy Street for a plateful and bottle in Greasy Pete's Alnight Restaurant and Minicab Service. Its patron, Crackadopolus, was dying from over-work. And his wife, the Emu, was being dragged to the grave with him. Greasy Pete hadn't slept since 1954. When he wasn't cooking kebabs he was driving his Zephyr round with another Greek in the back whose circumstances were slightly better than his. You had to knock to get in. Greasy Pete was at risk from the Irish and the Police. The Irish got in because he paid no attention to the licencing laws. The Police got in for the same reason.

A tap on the window and a net curtain was drawn aside. A

face like Omar Sharif's looks out. This was Crack's wife, the Emu. Jars of chilli steeped in sump-oil lined the counter. Courgettes pressed at the glass caught in that last terrifying rictus of freedom before they were plunged into the brine. All manner of offal in ulcerous acids was here. Most of these pickles only needed wiring up for conversion into batteries. Crack was engulfed in pork fumes somewhere behind them. The maroon flesh under his eyes extended into his emery stubble. Here comes another Retsina. The Emu clutches it in her claw together with two small dishes of *hummus*. She was so short she looked you straight in the eyes even though you were sitting down.

'Crack doesn't give her time to shave.'

'He doesn't love her,' I said.

I include a description of Crack's because it was in here almost exactly twenty years ago that one of us made a suggestion that was to have unexpectedly important consequences for my future. Why didn't we get out of London for a while and try and go on a holiday? We never thought we could get it together. But surprisingly we did. And that dreadful wet week up a hill in Ullswater became *Withnail and I*.

Meanwhile the sixties were falling to bits and we were back in Camden Town. Then something extraordinary happened. My companion got a job. It wasn't much as I remember. A bit of a shuffle round the provinces with Bernard Shaw. But it was work. And I was alone.

Worse was to come.

The Department of Health and Social Security suddenly decided to starve me to death. I was summoned to Victoria in a blizzard to explain what it was about my acting abilities that caused me to be unemployed for thirteen months. When I'd finished explaining a face behind an iron grid told me I wasn't getting the money.

'You're under review,' she said. 'Here's two quid.'

There was a certain amount of vocal coming from the other booths and the volume started going up in mine.

'I've been to drama school and haven't eaten anything,' I said.

She turned away and said, 'Eric,' and a huge black in a mackintosh appeared and told me to piss off.

By now most of the furniture was hocked and the premises were divided into two. A friend of David's with architectural leanings had converted the house into 'apartments'. This was achieved by nailing a hardboard door over the bottom of the stairs. He lived in the lower quarters. And I in the upper. Rarely did we speak.

Shall I ever forget that fearful January of 1969.

Snow piled at the kerbside like dirty laundry. A boot with a hole in it the size of a boiled egg. All day I would wander the boards saying, 'Not another day. Not another day.' And when the street lights came on, 'Not another night. Not another night.'

I had a packet of raisins and a tin of pilchards. Five bob and a face to feed. Often did I scuttle down to Camden Market looking for an abandoned vegetable. Here is a recipe for Turnip Biscuits:

Mix your flour, raisins and turnip together with a little milk pinched from someone's doorstep. And set aside. Break into the apartment downstairs and secure a knob of butter. (Swill his whisky, if there is any.) Return your pan to the heat. Add a pilchard. And cook till you smell it.

I had a lightbulb that travelled with me around the house. At night it would go on in the kitchen where I would sit in front of the oven watching it like a TV. At some suitable hour my bulb and I would go to bed. I slept at the top of the building overlooking the street. Outside a lamp post served electricity the colour of a wrecked tangerine.

I will not forget the silence of those endless winter nights. Albert Street shining and deaf under a fresh fall of snow. I used to look out of the window for a long time. Even lorries passed in silence. Sometimes somebody might go by with a dog. But more often than not they were alone.

Then the writ arrived. The rates. A pair of municipal eye-balls buried in blood pressure handed it across. 'The Justices require you to appear for a terminal shafting by specialists in Hampstead Magistrates' Court.' Back upstairs the street light was already on. The floorboards in the living room orange. Next thing I was on my knees staring at the hideous lamp and bleating at the sky.

'Give me a job. Anything. Anything.'

I prayed to the God of Equity and I prayed to the God of Christ. My forehead greeted the boards. I thought a weeping was imminent. It was the beginning of a laugh. I was so fucked it was inspiring. Whatever was in the Olivetti got dumped, and *Withnail* was begun. With no plot nor plan my intention was to write a sort of comic diary of my predicament. Unusually for me the ideas kept coming and organised themselves into a book. I wrote it fast at the kitchen table, and when it was finished it still made me laugh and I realised I had a problem. I wasn't worried about acting any more. I wanted to be a writer.

Fifteen years of shit queued instantly for negotiation. After ten years of almost continuous typing my only contribution to English letters was one published in the *Evening Standard*. It was about government manipulation of the media.

And now on to *Advertising*.

I generally try to avoid 'The World's Favourite Airline.' (British Airways isn't favourite with me because they've blocked off emergency exits to get in more seats.) Other than that I couldn't give one for any of them. They're all lousy and they're all the same, and the worse they get the more stupid becomes their advertising.

The 'Winged Gonad' must go to Air Canada. Their ad goes something like this. Couple of shots of a Boeing on a fly-by. Mango sunset and expensive clouds. Cut to the freshly polished hulk parked at some airport. Lights on. We don't see the passengers. We hear them. Apparently they're all gripped in some festivity and can't be persuaded to disembark. This nonsense is compounded by the appearance of a simpleton on the plane's doorstep putting out a pair of milk bottles. Then the Voice-over. 'Air Canada.' And in tones like a pause during oral sex, 'Flights So Good You Won't Wanna Get Off.'

Well I've flown Air Canada and I can tell you I couldn't wait to sprint down the fucking gangplank. I've flown thousands and thousands of miles in aeroplanes, and I've never been in a landed aircraft and seen anyone, ever, who didn't want to *get off*.

We got on in Sydney late Monday afternoon. *How to Get Ahead in Advertising* was back on the menu. I was going to have to do something about this end of the introduction, and it was difficult because I was tired out and still didn't feel well from the holiday. Writing isn't pleasant and I had no ideas. I always feel dizzy before I write. It isn't easy to explain. Curiously a fear of flying gets near to it. Strapped in and waiting for take off. They've just gone through that routine about the exits and the water-wings and suddenly *you* and seventy tons of kerosene are hurtling forward at two hundred miles an hour. Should you find this alarming, 'You might care to have a look at the Safety Card in the seat pocket in front of you.'

I gave it a wide-eye once and couldn't believe what I was looking at. Drawings of people getting into life-jackets with *smiles* on their faces. Thirty-nine thousand feet, the starboard engine's on fire, and they're getting into their jackets grinning!

This of course is an understandable distortion of reality. (Drawings of passengers trying to get into the luggage racks wouldn't do.) What *How to Get Ahead in Advertising* attempts to explore is a more insidious sort of lying.

Right on cue here comes a trolley full of newspapers. I select yesterday's *Sunday Telegraph* for a perusal of what's happening in wonderland.

Page One.

Apparently escalating inflation and the biggest trade deficit England's ever seen are, according to the Chancellor of the Exchequer, 'symptoms of our success.' My lips move involuntarily as I try to come to terms with this horse shit. But that means that countries with no inflation, and no trade deficit, say Japan, are *unsuccessful*?

Outside my house in London is a telegraph pole. Half-way up it someone has nailed a notice to the effect that if your dog poops itself around here, 'You Will Be Subject To A Fifty Pound Fine By Order Of The Bla, Bla.' Naturally around the base of the pole is about three hundred quid's worth of dog shit. (I estimate revenue from the entire street in the thousands.) So what is the purpose of this prominent yellow declaration? Presumably it is based on the assumption that if you keep them looking up at the notice, they won't look down and see the shit.

Fifteen billion pounds in the red is simply *not* important. What *is* important is the 'Economic Miracle'.

Two of my favourite fictional heroes are Danes. One's obvious and the other is a ten-year-old kid in a crowd. 'Look at the King! Look at the King! Look at his horrible old hairy bum! The King has got no clothes!' Policemen who used to look like humans, and who now look like the front of Range Rovers, rush out and bash the little bastard insensible. And the naked continue on their way.

Some fucking fairy tale. Don't look down.

Propaganda is everywhere. It begins with the Bunnies and their Kingdoms of Heaven, and will undoubtably end with the kind of 'peace' we consider worthy of this planet by making atomic bombs. 'Bombs Is Peace. Bombs Is Peace.' Believe it. I personally never trust a vegetarian in a fur coat. Nor do I any longer believe in the 'Kingdom of Heaven.' If Heaven exists, which I doubt, it is almost certain to be a republic. The reason the Bible calls Heaven a kingdom is because it was hacked under the auspicies of kings who wanted to get in on the act. The reason newspapers print lies is because they are hacked under the auspicies of Government who also want in on the act.

It's not by accident that the editors of our three most popular newspapers received Government-initiated honours. Not an accident that a majority of British newspapers are filth.

With a few exceptions newspapers in the United Kingdom are an affront to the notion of a decent society.

But wait a minute. Hasn't our most senior politician decreed that 'society' doesn't exist? What are we all living in then? I reach for my pocket OED. 'Society . . . the system or mode of life adopted by a body of individuals for the purpose of harmonious existence . . .'

Christ she's right!

One only needs peek into the nation's biggest-selling ink for proof.

We live in a land of Liars, Scroungers, Swines, Cheats, Pimps, Monsters, Muggers, Ogres, Poofs, Bastards, Micks, Wops, Wogs, Argies, Tarts, Whips, Commies, Chinks, Intellectuals, Mollesters, Smellers, Exposers, Students, Sadists, The Labour Party, and Poisoned Frog Cheese.

Plus the 'Economic Miracle'. Tits and TV.

The particular waste of paper I'm referring to considers a 'balanced view' a big pair of tits given equal prominence towards the camera. This 'Fun Lover' was honoured by Downing Street. Our Prime Minister gave its editor a knighthood.

'MUM OF SHAME.'

It's not an accident that the England depicted in these dangerous comics would frighten Hieronymus Bosch. This rubbish serves two functions. First, attempt to lower the standards of everything to a level at which the Executive wishes to operate. Indoctrinate them to the lousy. Get them comfortable with lies. Wipe out the notion of ethics. If this can be achieved it becomes easier to camouflage the duplicity and ever-evaporating morals of Government. Second, sell them a land of perpetual catastrophe. The more crime the better. Far from having any deleterious effect crime is good for authority. Throw a rock through their window, then knock on the door and sell them all a burglar alarm. Sell them fear and they'll buy the bombs. Sell them Sodom and they'll howl for Police. And this administration is going to need all the police it can get.

Mrs Thatcher's 'Economic Miracle' is a fantasy. A sham

underwritten by grubby swindlers who increasingly impose upon our media either by bullying it, bribing it, or buying it. The Miracle is propaganda. The Miracle is asset stripping. The Miracle is North Sea Oil. And the tragedy is that this Prime Minister and her mendacious confederacy should have coincided with it.

This is becoming a horrible little bugger of an island. Our freedoms perish daily, replaced by a spurious notion of 'liberty' that is in reality greed. Our society is being torn up by a Parliament of shouting dopes, mesmerised in delinquent passion for coin that seemingly can never be gratified. It has always been the expertise of the elite to flog what's good for them as good for everybody. And sure, there may be a few bob more in the average voter's pocket. But this is going to end in calamity. (Disaster will be selective, of course, and apply only to the majority.) For the rest there won't be enough Concords to go around. When this squandering and selfishness finally self-destruct, when the oil and everything else embezzled from this island are hocked and gone, the 'Miracle' will cease, and those walking upon our foreign-owned waters will fall in.

But unhappily not for long. Horrible yakking heads will resurface almost immediately to deal with the 'crisis'.

'NOW MORE THAN EVER THE COUNTRY NEEDS STRONG GOVERNMENT!' screams the nearest Wipe. 'THE PEOPLE DEMAND ACTION TO SAVE THEM FROM CATASTROPHE!'

No problem.

Having delivered the rock here comes the burglar alarm.

1: All natural resources are to be privately owned.
2: Businessmen are to be free. 'Self Government in Business.'
3: The social structure of society is sanctified. The middle class are the backbone of the State.
4: Employers have practically complete control over workmen in regard to wages, hours and conditions. Collective bargaining is abolished. Strikes are illegal. Trade unions forbidden.

5: Control is completely from on top. The leaders decide all things as they see fit. Central government controls all local government.

6: There can be no freedom of speech, of assembly, of writing. Anyone may criticise the government who is not afraid to go to prison.

7: Socialism is the major enemy. There can be no such thing as equality. The 'broad masses' are fools and must be duped and led to meet the purposes of the elite.

8: All sciences and 'culture' must be co-ordinated to serve the purposes of the leader. Propaganda is the method. Propaganda knows neither right nor wrong. Neither truth nor falsehood. But only what it wants . . .

Any of that ring a bell? I copied it out of *The Spirit and Structure of German Facism* by Robert Brady, Professor of Economics at the University of California. It's his summary of the 'Nazi' system of government published in 1937.

I think we're well on the way. As I write, truth, *truth*, mind you, in circumstances inimical to the Executive is to become a criminal offence. (See 6 above.) Our Home Secretary soothingly assures us this flamboyant legislation is a big step-forward in the 'liberalisation of government'.

'THICK FOG IN THE CHANNEL, CONTINENT CUT OFF FROM BRITAIN,' as the *Daily Express* once foamed. Those same morbid clouds are congealing over England again. Fasten seat belts, Ladies and Gentlemen, we are preparing for our final descent.

They're about to sell us the rain we drink. Rain made out of 'water' (T.M.) They're about to sell us our electricity industry that we've paid for a million times. Flog off the volts at knock-down prices. But tax off our ass to save the nukes. Apparently Private Enterprise can't-quite-stretch to the 'Nuclear Miracle' (once proffered to the masses as 'Power Too Cheap To Meter'), now mysteriously 'too expensive' for the punters to buy.

Remember the 'Atom Miracle' of 1953? 'THE WORLD'S FIRST

CIVIL NUCLEAR POWER STATION!' (Slung up in reality because the Americans wouldn't give us any bombs.) Remember Calder Hall? Or was it Seascale? Or Windscale? Or Sellafield? Every time the bastard had an accident they changed its name.

Our country is being managed like a deceitful little shop, and a permed figure lurks behind the 'Special Offers' with eagle-eyes on the till. Our gorgeous little island is up for sale. Tomorrow its museums, its lakes, its mines, and its parks. For be assured these bargains will never cease.

In *How to Get Ahead in Advertising* all my leading character wants to do is sell the public boils.

Some fucking fairy tale. Don't look down.

We shall shortly be arriving at Heathrow.

B.R. January 1989

Withnail and I

I. INT. APARTMENT. DAY.

*Low-quality daylight . . . dawn light . . . here comes some music
. . . King Curtis on sax . . . a magnificent rendition of 'A Whiter
Shade of Pale' . . . so sweet . . . so sour . . . this is beautiful.*

WITHNAIL AND I

*In big letters as the solo begins. Principal titles will continue over
this room. Despite the squalor the room is furnished with antiques
. . . heirlooms and other quality stuff . . . an indescribable
mélange of stuff crowds a low table. A large Victorian globe of the
world soars above bacon rinds. Objets d'art and breakfast remains
compete for space.*

*Dostoyevsky described hell as perhaps nothing more than a room
with a chair in it. This room has several chairs. A young man sits in
one. He isn't comfortable. He is leaning forward. He is scrutinising
his thumbs. He is wired. Now he's lighting a cigarette. Now
nothing is moving but cigarette smoke. And no sound other than the
beautiful lachrymose saxophone.*

The man in the chair is MARWOOD. *Twenty-five years old.
Milk white with insomnia. Glasses like Lennon's and a sweet face
behind them. Seventy-five per cent good looks and the rest is
anxiety. This is a long haul with unspecified destination. Only
thing certain is there are still hours to go. Hours and hours have
stagnated in here. Drifting in cigarette smoke and settling with the
dust.*

*And everything looks ill. The walls and furniture look ill.
Daylight looks ill. He exhales a huge bouquet of smoke. It's blue.
Shifts again and runs hands through his hair. It's black and could
do with a dose of Vosene.*

3

MARWOOD *reaches for a bottle of beer instead. Swallows a stale inch with eyes on the move . . . they navigate the globe and it seems to disgust him. Keep moving and good God in heaven is* this *what he sees?*

2. P.O.V. MARWOOD.
A kitchen extends off the living room. But much worse. The living room doesn't have a sink. This room does and it looks like it's vomited. The unwashed and the unwashable are stacked to the height of the taps. Every horizontal surface is covered in naso-visual horror. Here are the remains of fish suppers and the newspapers in which they were dispensed. Here are saucepans filled with unspeakable liquids. Here are empty wine bottles and dead flowers. Roses in black water like knuckles of congealed blood. Here is a frying pan driven vertically *with a partially fried egg still attached . . .*

3. INT. KITCHEN. APARTMENT. DAY.
The view stops MARWOOD *in his tracks. He's come in here and brought the titles with him. He stares, as though witnessing this panorama of degradation for the first time.*

Something must be done to maintain equilibrium. His eyes settle on a kettle. A decision is taken. Plunging at the sink he fills it with water and slams his kettle on the gas.

A hypnotic blue flame circles the kettle. For a moment it demands his attention. But this thing's beginning to freak him out . . . the flame is devouring all the oxygen supplies . . . like the whole fucking house is having an asthma attack.

No air in here and he heads back to the living room. But the camera doesn't bother to follow (it's seen this journey a hundred times before). It stays here with the kettle and flame and lets him pace in the distance of the apartment.

There he goes past the globe. And here he is coming back again. Now he's looking in the mirror. Now re-observing his thumbs. Looks like he's taking his pulse (but maybe that's an illusion). Now suddenly another decision is made and he stubs his cigarette . . . scarf on . . . long black overcoat on . . . some kind of limit seems to

4

*have been reached. Now he's on his way through the kitchen door
and the music and camera must follow.*

4. INT. STAIRWAY. APARTMENT. DAY.
*Too dark to see anything much out here. Boots clatter on carpetless
stairs.* MARWOOD *reaches the bottom and knocks on a door.*
MARWOOD: I'm going for a cup of tea . . . (*Silence.*) D'you
    want one? (*Silence.*) D'you want a cup of tea, Withnail?
WITHNAIL (*O.S.*): No.
    MARWOOD *is already on the move. Motoring on bile he
    descends more stairs. Hits a front door and slams the music
    behind him.*

5. EXT. STREET. CAMDEN TOWN. DAWN.
*A boarded-up warehouse opposite. A clapped-out Jaguar parked
outside a line of old dwellings.* MARWOOD *emerges from one of
them. Fills his lungs before heading up the street.*
MARWOOD (*V.O. – playback*): . . . perhaps thirteen million
    people in London. And if they all go once a day, that
    means end to end there'd be enough shit to stretch from
    here to Casablanca . . .

6. EXT. ALLEYWAY. CAMDEN TOWN. DAWN.
*The street lights are still on. Utterly dismal. A carbon copy of a
day.* MARWOOD *scurries and the camera hurries with him. Their
combined speed puts the dripping alley in a blur.*
MARWOOD (*V.O.*): I'm not working it out now. I'd done that
    before with Withnail. Also computed the Dresden route
    via Cologne. And Moscow in a day and a half . . .
    *Still hanging in as close as it can the camera turns a corner and
    now they're under a railway bridge. Rain hangs like dirty
    tinsel. The area is as shabby as the weather.*
MARWOOD (*V.O.*): Thirteen million people in London, and
    Withnail's gotta be the only one who would bother to
    work that out. Why would he work that out? The bastard
    must be unique.
    An old HEAP *under the bridge is selling newspapers. His face*

*glows in the light of a carbide lamp. A billboard announces
that a 'Vicar Batters Old Woman to Death in Sex Outrage'.
Before* MARWOOD *realises it he has stopped to buy a
newspaper.*

MARWOOD: *Evening News* please.

A good middle-class accent. Blank response from the HEAP.
Evening News please.

OLD HEAP: It's Sunday morning, mate . . .

7. INT. WANKER'S CAFÉ. CAMDEN TOWN. DAY.
*A dozen eggs billow in a massive pan. This is full-frontal frying
and you can hear them flap. A spatula goes in and a pair are hauled
out and slid on to a plate. Big close up it crosses the café revealing*
MARWOOD *as it passes.*

More news now as MARWOOD *scans a rag. Here are murderers
and muggers and photographs of tits and advertisements for trusses
and John and Yoko and maniacal vicars and brassières and atomic
bombs and Vietnam and pillage and thousands on the rampage.*

Wide-eyed with shock MARWOOD *lowers his newspaper.
Practically everybody else in the dump is behind one. This café is a
hovel. Grease and fumes and ketchup bottles with blackened
foreskins. Some horrible faces in here.* MARWOOD *watches an old
woman eating – her fried-egg sandwich ruptures. Loathing and
fascination. Loathing wins it and he turns away. Comes face to
face with 'Why I Did it – Mother of Eleven Tells All'. There is no
escape . . .*

MARWOOD (*V.O.*): Thirteen million people have to cope with
this? And vicars and All Bran and rape? And I'm sitting in
this fucking shack and I can't cope with Withnail? I must
be out of my mind. I must go home at once and discuss his
problems in depth.

8. INT. STAIRWAY/LIVING ROOM. APARTMENT. DAY.
MARWOOD *blunders upstairs. Passes the bathroom door on his
way. As he does so a man appears. Thirty years old. Pale as an
oven-ready chicken. His hair is wet. The eyes have practically
vanished under mauve lids. But the face is shaved and has dignity.*

6

So do the clothes. He wears a tweed overcoat. Corduroy trousers and brogues. There's class here somewhere. His name is WITHNAIL.

WITHNAIL: I have some extremely distressing news . . .
His voice has been to Oxford and is deadly with sincerity.

MARWOOD: I don't wanna hear it. I don't wanna hear anything.
Back to the living room. Nothing has changed except that it's now filled with steam. Neither seems to notice and MARWOOD *doesn't remember he put a kettle on. He hot-foots it in and the pacing recommences. This time with an intensity that forewarns some sort of crisis.*

MARWOOD: My God, it's a nightmare out there. I tell you, it's a fucking nightmare.

WITHNAIL: We've just run out of wine. What are we gonna do about it?

MARWOOD: I dunno. I don't know. I don't feel good. I feel like my liver just stopped.
MARWOOD*'s glasses mist with condensation. He pounds up the carpet wringing anxiety out of his newspaper . . . sees his reflection in a mirror. Muscles earthquake and he gets a rush.*

MARWOOD: Jesus Christ. I think I've overdone it. I think I've overdosed. My thumbs have gone weird. I'm in the middle of a fucking overdose . . .

WITHNAIL: Give me that newspaper . . .
He grabs the paper and collapses on the sofa. MARWOOD *is still going up a hill.*

MARWOOD: . . . my heart's beating like a fucked clock. I feel dreadful. I feel fucking dreadful . . .

WITHNAIL: So do I. So does everybody. Look at my tongue. It's wearing a yellow sock. Sit down, for Christ's sake. What's the matter with you? Eat some sugar.
He fights the newspaper into shape. MARWOOD *gathers his senses and quicks it into the kitchen. Begins a frenzied search for a drinking receptacle. There's only a soup bowl. He's transferring sugar when* WITHNAIL *appears through the steam.*

7

WITHNAIL: Listen to this. 'Curse of the Supermen . . .'
WITHNAIL is reading from the paper with a disturbing looking grin.
'I took drugs to win medal, says top athlete, Jeff Wode.'
MARWOOD: Where's the coffee?
WITHNAIL: 'In a world exclusive interview, thirty-three year-old shot putter, Jeff Wode, who weighs three hundred and seventeen pounds, admitted taking massive doses of anabolic steroids, drugs banned in sport.'
MARWOOD doesn't want to listen. Tangents off looking for coffee.
'He used to get in bad tempers and act daft, says his wife. He used to pick on me. Now he's stopped, he's much better in our sex life, and in our general life.'
A jar of Maxwell House on the table. MARWOOD grabs it and they return to the kitchen. Wode has excited WITHNAIL's imagination.
Jesus Christ, this huge thatched head with its sideboards and cannon ball is now considered sane. Jeff Wode is feeling better. And is now prepared to step back into society and start tossing his orb about.
MARWOOD shakes coffee from the jar and mixes it with his finger. Grabbing a magazine he uses it to insulate the white-hot kettle.
Look at him. Look at Jeff Wode.
MARWOOD pours water into the soup bowl. Is forced to look at a face with hair sprouting from the nose and ears – sideboards exiting from the nostrils.
His ear lobes must weigh a pound and a half each . . .
MARWOOD: Take him away. I don't wanna see him.
WITHNAIL: Imagine the size of his balls.
The kettle returns to the gas. Jeff Wode is fascinating WITHNAIL.
Imagine getting into a fight with the fucker.
Clutching his soup bowl MARWOOD pushes past into the living room.
MARWOOD: Please. I don't feel good.

WITHNAIL: That's what you'd say. But that wouldn't wash with *Jeff*. He'd like a bit of pleading. Adds spice to it. In fact, he'd probably tell you what he was gonna do before he did it. 'I'm gonna *pull your head off*.' 'No, please. Please don't pull my head off.' 'I'm gonna *pull your head off*, because I don't *like* your head . . .'

WITHNAIL stops mid-sentence. Stares with accelerating indignation.

Have you got soup?

MARWOOD sits and begins sipping coffee from the edge of his bowl.

Why don't I get any soup?

MARWOOD: Coffee.

WITHNAIL: Well why don't you use a *cup* like any other human being?

MARWOOD: Why don't you *wash up* occasionally like any other human being?

Before the words have left his mouth MARWOOD realises he's made a mistake. If it is possible for a face as white as WITHNAIL's to pale the moment is now. Crumpling his newspaper he marches forward. In the interests of safety MARWOOD rises to his feet.

WITHNAIL: How dare you? How *dare* you? How dare you call *me* inhumane?

MARWOOD: I didn't call you inhumane. You merely imagined that. Calm down.

WITHNAIL: Right you *fucker*. I'm gonna do the washing up.

The crisis has focused. MARWOOD moves in to prevent a development.

MARWOOD: You can't. It's impossible. I swear to you. I've looked into it.

A cross between a scuffle and a waltz. MARWOOD leading in both.

Listen to me. *Listen.* There are *things* in there. There's a tea bag growing. You haven't slept for sixty hours, you're in no state to tackle it. Wait for the morning, and we'll go in together.

9

WITHNAIL: This *is* the morning. Stand aside.
Rolling up the sleeve of his overcoat WITHNAIL *barges into the steam.* MARWOOD *follows, issuing warnings.*

MARWOOD: You don't understand. I think there may be something *living* in there. I think there's something alive . . .
It's difficult to see what's happening. But WITHNAIL *is in possession of the Fairy Liquid bottle and is wielding it like a gun.*

WITHNAIL: What d'you mean, a *rat*?

MARWOOD: Possibly. It's possible.

WITHNAIL: Then the *fucker* will *rue* the *day*.
Firing his bottle WITHNAIL *plunges at the sink. Both taps go on and there's a clatter of activity.*
Christ Almighty.
And he staggers back clutching a saucepan filled with pungent brown fluids.
Sinew in nicotine base.
A fascination for the unclean drives MARWOOD *towards the visuals.*
Keep back. Keep back. The entire sink's gone rotten. I don't know what's in here.
A space for the saucepan is cleared. MARWOOD *stares at it while* WITHNAIL *pours water from the kettle and envelops himself in a cloud of super-heated steam. A volcanic growl comes from the fog. Bellowing loudly,* WITHNAIL *passes at speed with his hand in the air.*

MARWOOD: I told you. You've been bitten.

WITHNAIL: *Burnt. Burnt.* The fucking kettle's on fire.

MARWOOD: There's something floating up.
WITHNAIL paces back into the kitchen. A voice laced with revenge.

WITHNAIL: Fork it.

MARWOOD: No. No. I don't wanna touch it.

WITHNAIL: You must. You must. That shit'll bore through the glaze. We'll never be able to use the dinner service again.

He tugs at a drawer stuffed with domestic items. Produces a tool.

Here. Get it with the pliers.

MARWOOD: No. No. Give me the gloves.

Rubber gloves are handed across. WITHNAIL *stares as they go on.*

WITHNAIL: That's right. Put on the gloves. Don't attempt anything without the gloves.

Defying the view MARWOOD *goes in. Starts probing into the depths.*

MARWOOD: There's a boiled egg in here.

WITHNAIL: This is too much to bear.

An explosion of stagnant chilli and he reels back from the sink. What is it? What have you *found*?

MARWOOD: Matter.

WITHNAIL: *Matter*? Where's it coming from?

WITHNAIL'*s eyes prod as he forces himself forward for an exposé.*

MARWOOD: Don't come. Don't look. I'm dealing with it.

WITHNAIL: I think we've been in here too long. I feel unusual. I think we should go outside.

MARWOOD *is diving for the foundations. Half a loaf comes out. Then other things. Both are dumbstruck. There is nothing they can do. Very slowly the image begins to dissolve . . .*

MARWOOD (*V.O.*): . . . a Chinese take-away was the foundation to this pile of horror . . . One flattened ball of pork (which the inventor may, in wide-eyed innocence, have conceived as *sweet*) . . .

9. EXT. REGENT'S PARK. LONDON. DAY.

MARWOOD (*V.O.*): . . . but could not, in his wildest Chinese nightmare, have appreciated what the addition of the word *sour* might entail . . .

Black railings against mist. Drizzle clings to the trees. This is a section of the park bordering on the zoo. Half a dozen wolves are hanging about, looking pissed off. As bored with looking at WITHNAIL *and* MARWOOD *as the two men are*

11

bored with looking at them. WITHNAIL *and* MARWOOD
*turn away and start walking down a path. Overcoats
wrapped around them and arms wrapped around the coats.*

WITHNAIL: This is ridiculous. Look at me. I'm thirty in a
month. And I've got a *sole* flapping off my shoe.

MARWOOD: It'll get better. It has to . . .

WITHNAIL'*s expression is a mixture of vitamin-lack and
cynicism.*

WITHNAIL: Easy enough for you to say 'lovey', you've had an
audition . . . Why can't I have an audition?

*An audition? Can these two wrecks be actors? Evidently they
are.*

It's ridiculous. I've been to drama school. I'm good
looking. I tell you, I've a fuck sight more talent than half
the rubbish that gets on television. Why can't I get on
television?

MARWOOD *has clearly listened to this before. He turns away
cold.*

MARWOOD: I dunno. It'll happen . . .

WITHNAIL: Will it? That's what you say. The only
programme I'm likely to get on is the fucking news.

The assessment is probably correct. Unlikely anyone would let
WITHNAIL *loose in a television studio. Much less pay him to
be there.*

WITHNAIL: I tell you, I can't take much more of this, I'm
going to crack.

MARWOOD: I'm in the same boat . . .

WITHNAIL (*muttering*): Yeah, yeah.

Conversation blows away in the wind.

WITHNAIL: I feel sick as a pike. I'm gonna have to sit down.

10. EXT. PIAZZA. REGENT'S PARK. DAY.

A church bell tolls somewhere. Misery times eight equals Sunday.
MARWOOD *is squinting at his reflection in a puddle. Like an
Escher drawing.* WITHNAIL *sits shivering on a bench like he's
been there all night.*

MARWOOD: You know what we should do . . .

And he walks back to join WITHNAIL. *Sits when he fancies it.*

I say, you know what we should do?

WITHNAIL: How can I possibly know what *we* should do? *What* should we do?

MARWOOD: Get out of it for a while. Get into the countryside and rejuvenate.

WITHNAIL: Rejuvenate? I'm in a *park* and I'm practically dead. What good's the countryside? What time is it?

MARWOOD: Eight.

WITHNAIL: Four hours to opening, God help us.

WITHNAIL *adjusts his massive tartan scarf.*

Have we got any embrocation?

MARWOOD: What for?

WITHNAIL: To *rub on us* you fool. We can cover ourselves in Deep Heat and get up against a radiator. Keep ourselves alive till twelve.

WITHNAIL *suddenly spits with great violence. An oyster is born. He observes it in a great state of partial hypnosis.*

Jesus. Look at that. Apart from a raw potato, that's the only solid to pass my lips in the last sixty hours. I must be ill.

11. INT. LIVING ROOM. APARTMENT. DAY.

The shutters are open and WITHNAIL *stares across to the partially demolished building opposite. The site is silent but has a giant crane sporting one of those huge iron bash-balls on the end of a chain.*

MARWOOD (*V.O.*): Even a stopped clock gives the right time twice a day, and for once I am inclined to believe Withnail is right . . .

WITHNAIL *looks unstable and grimy with the hue of wet cement. Wears his overcoat and a sock. Entire corpse smeared with embrocation . . .*

. . . we are indeed drifting into the arena of the unwell. What we need is harmony . . . fresh air and stuff like that . . .

MARWOOD *sits on the sofa. Smokes a cigarette and puts*

13

thoughts into a battered notebook.

WITHNAIL: Wasn't much in the tube. There's nothing left for
you.

He throws MARWOOD *the empty tube and draws his overcoat
around him.*

MARWOOD: Why don't you ask your father for some money?
If we had some money we could go away.

WITHNAIL: Why don't you ask *your* father? How can it be so
cold in here? It's like *Greenland* in here. We've got to get
some booze. It's the only solution to this intense cold.

Donning a boot WITHNAIL *begins to patrol. There is a
distinct possibility the fuses are going to blow. Muscles are
white molars are grinding. A wild look in his eyes. And he's
put on the rubber gloves.*

Something's got to be done. We can't go on like this. I'm a
trained actor reduced to the status of a *bum*. Look at us.
Nothing that reasonable members of society demand as
their rights. No fridges. No televisions. No phones.

MARWOOD *isn't really listening. Continues to write in his
book.*

Much more of this, I'm gonna apply for Meals on Wheels.

MARWOOD: What happened to your cigar commercial?

WITHNAIL: That's what I wanna know. What happened to my
cigar commercial? What's happened to my *agent*? The
bastard must have died.

MARWOOD: September. It's a bad patch.

WITHNAIL: Rubbish. I haven't seen Gielgud down the
Labour Exchange.

WITHNAIL *is beginning to look like some minor character
from a nineteenth-century Russian novel. Withnailovich.
Incidental to the plot.*

Why doesn't he retire? (*Grabs newspaper.*) Look at this
little bastard. 'Boy lands plum role for top Italian
director.' Course he does. Probably on a tenner a day.
And I know what for. Two pound ten a tit and a fiver for
his arse . . .

MARWOOD *has had enough of it. Stubs his cigarette and*

walks away. WITHNAIL *is becoming unusual. He follows into the kitchen. Looks with disgust at* MARWOOD *who's got a fork going into a honey pot. Muttering invective about the temperature* WITHNAIL *poles off for his clothes. A thought suddenly occurs and he turns accusingly.*

WITHNAIL: Have you been at the controls?

MARWOOD: What are you talking about?

WITHNAIL: The *thermostats*. What have you *done* to them?

MARWOOD: Haven't touched them.

WITHNAIL: Then why has my head gone numb?

Some sort of climax approaches.

I must have some booze. I *demand* to have some booze.

His eyes sweep the room. Home in on a can of Ronsonol.

MARWOOD: I wouldn't drink that if I was you.

WITHNAIL: Why not? Why not?

MARWOOD: Because I don't advise it. Even wankers on the site wouldn't drink that. That's worse than meths.

WITHNAIL: Nonsense. This is a far superior drink to meths. The wankers don't drink it because they can't afford it.

Levering the cap with his teeth he tears it off. The mouth opens with a bilious cackle and throwing his head back WITHNAIL *downs the petrol in one. A falsetto whine follows as he comes up fighting for air.* MARWOOD *looks worried.*

Have we got any more?

MARWOOD *looks more worried. Shakes his head and steps back. This drug-crazed fool in overcoat and underpants seems poised to kill.*

Liar. What's in your tool box?

MARWOOD: We have nothing. Sit down.

WITHNAIL: Liar. You've got anti-freeze.

One comes on and one backs off. The latter with certain urgency.

MARWOOD: You bloody fool. You should never mix your drinks!

The joke is an accident. It stops WITHNAIL *in his tracks. This is evidently the funniest thing he's ever heard. Barking with hysteria he staggers forward. Suddenly he's down. He*

15

throws up on MARWOOD's *shoes. However, we'll be spared visuals of this incident.*

Mercifully, all we'll see is his reaction. The victim may mutter 'Oh, God, no.' And on the other hand he may not. Some music gets in here. A single bleak electric guitar.

12. INT. KITCHEN. APARTMENT. DAY.

The music will continue until I tell it to stop. MARWOOD *has his boots on the kitchen table. He's scrubbed them and applies perfume. The door bell rings and he freezes. As he moves he knocks the essence of petunia all over his trousers! No time to swear because he's heading for the living room.* WITHNAIL *is stretched along the couch under his overcoat. He squints up with equal alarm.*

MARWOOD *crouches in the window. A wing mirror from a motor-bike is bolted to the balcony outside. It affords a view of the front step. A bald and affluent-looking man lurking.*

MARWOOD: It's him . . .

WITHNAIL: We're out . . .

MARWOOD: I know we are . . .

13. EXT. STREET. CAMDEN TOWN. DAY.

Not a lot has changed since MARWOOD *was last in the street. More people about. Mainly Irish wankers hanging about the tube station for no apparent reason. Too daft or too broke to care that it's past opening time. Though they both look utterly wasted, the chuck up seems to have improved* WITHNAIL. *He counts change as they scuttle along.*

WITHNAIL: All right, this is the plan. We'll get in there and get wrecked. Then we'll eat a *pork pie*. Then we'll go home and drop a couple of Surmontil 50s each. That means we'll miss out Monday, but come up smiling Tuesday morning.

Were this a new theory of evolution the answer would be the same.

MARWOOD: It's a good idea . . .

WITHNAIL: Nothing ever happens on Mondays. I hate bastard Mondays.

16

14. INT. MOTHER BLACK CAP. PUBLIC HOUSE. DAY.
This is an Irish pub. It's filling up in direct proportion to the emptying of the churches. The bar is full of men. Only two women in here and they look like men. Faces like rotten beetroots. One has a tuft of carrot-coloured hair. Everybody here has one thing in common. They have come in here to get drunk. It's a horrible place. Shit-coloured Formica. Carpet like the surface of a road. The atmosphere is rank with smoke and Irish accent. WITHNAIL *leads the way to the bar and is served at once.*

WITHNAIL: Two large gins. Two pints of cider. Ice in the cider.

> WITHNAIL *sits on a stool.* MARWOOD *supports himself on the bar, fiddling in the ashtray and rediscovering a thought.*

MARWOOD: If my father was loaded, I'd ask him for some money.

WITHNAIL: And if your father was my father, you wouldn't get it.

> *A packet of Gauloises comes out. And here come the pair of gins.*

Chin. Chin.

> *These boys are purely medicinal. Down in one. On to the ciders. Enough time passes for them both to get through half a glass.*

MARWOOD: What about what's his name?

> MARWOOD *is in the middle of a conversation that never started.*

WITHNAIL: What about him?

MARWOOD: Why don't you give him a call?

WITHNAIL: What for?

> MARWOOD *gestures to a phone on the wall behind* WITHNAIL's *head. If* WITHNAIL *weren't so wasted he'd perhaps focus the conversation.*

MARWOOD: Ask him about his house.

WITHNAIL: You want me to call what's his name and ask him about his house?

MARWOOD: Why not?

WITHNAIL: All right. What's his number?

MARWOOD *is so spaced he has to think a moment before replying.*

MARWOOD: I've no idea. I've never met him.

WITHNAIL: Neither have I. Who the *fuck* are you talking about?

MARWOOD: Your relative. With the house in the country.

WITHNAIL: Monty? Uncle Monty?

MARWOOD: That's him. That's the one. Get the Jag fixed up and spend a week in the country.

If the phone were any further away the chances would be slim. But WITHNAIL *can almost reach it without getting off his stool.*

WITHNAIL: All right. Give us a tanner, and I'll give him a bell.

If muscles worked MARWOOD *would smile. He pulls a ten bob note.*

MARWOOD: Get a couple more in. I'm going for a slash . . .

WITHNAIL *is putting in another order as* MARWOOD *makes his way across the bar. An enormous* WANKER *is sitting by the lavatory door. He's had a few. He's togged out in a Burton's and wearing size twelve black platformed boots. Obviously fashion conscious. As* MARWOOD *passes, he looks up.*

WANKER: Ponce.

MARWOOD *registers the address but doesn't acknowledge it. Navigates into the Gents' with no visible manifestations of terror.*

15. INT. GENTS' LAVATORIES. DAY.

MARWOOD (*V.O. and playback*): I could hardly piss straight with fear. Here was a man with three-quarters of an inch of brain who had taken a dislike to me. What had I done to offend him? I don't consciously offend big men like this. This one has a definite imbalance of hormone in him. Get any more masculine than him and you'd have to live up a tree.

MARWOOD *is approaching a swoon. He leans into the wall*

18

manufacturing sweat. 'I FUCK ARSES' is etched into the
plaster with dedication. His senses capsize at the implications
of the threat.
I fuck arses? Who fucks arses? Maybe *he* fucks arses.
Maybe he's written this in some moment of drunken
sincerity? I'm in considerable danger in here. I must get
out of here at once . . .
Following his own advice he zips and beats it through the
door.

16. INT. MOTHER BLACK CAP. PUBLIC HOUSE. DAY.
The pair of size twelve black platform boots are still in situ.
WANKER: Perfumed ponce.
    MARWOOD keeps walking and arrives at the bar.
    WITHNAIL greets him with a puckered smile.
WITHNAIL: You'll be pleased to hear, Monty has invited us
    for drinks . . .
MARWOOD: Balls to Monty. We're getting out.
WITHNAIL: Balls to Monty? I've just spent an hour flattering
    the bugger.
    Two pints have just appeared. WITHNAIL's *interest is with*
    them.
MARWOOD: There's one over there doesn't like the perfume.
    A big one.
    WITHNAIL manipulates a mouthful of cider. Swallows it and
    turns.
MARWOOD (*cont.*): Don't look, don't look. We're in danger.
    We gotta get out.
WITHNAIL: What are you talking about?
MARWOOD: I've been called a ponce.
    More pissed than sensible WITHNAIL *swivels boldly on the*
    bar.
WITHNAIL: What *fucker* said that?
    The fucker who said it has just put full weight on to his size
    twelves. And they're coming across the room.
    Intuitively WITHNAIL *realises this is him. A profound*
    change in his expression.

This man is huge. Red hair. Face and neck peppered with stubble and bright red with drink. At the end of his arms are arguably the biggest hands in existence. Both bramble-patched with hair.

As the WANKER *approaches* WITHNAIL *attempts to dissociate himself from* MARWOOD. *But the technique is totally unsuccessful and* WITHNAIL *faces the* WANKER.

WANKER: I called him a ponce. And now I'm calling you one. Ponce.

WITHNAIL: Would you like a drink?

No he wouldn't. He's had ten pints. That's why he's over here. He grabs WITHNAIL's *tartan scarf and renders it unto the floor.*

WANKER: What's your name? McFuck?

A couple of days pass while WITHNAIL *searches for a suitable reply.*

WITHNAIL: I have a heart condition.

The bastard is working himself into some kind of violent lather.

I have a heart condition.

If you hit me it's murder.

WANKER: I'll murder the paira ya.

His eyes alternate between them. Pork ugly. Organs of a brute. WITHNAIL's *voice comes out in a curiously high-pitched whisper.*

WITHNAIL: My wife is having a baby.

Both WITHNAIL *and* MARWOOD *are paralysed with panic. Both are speechless with fear. They stand to attention in front of the* WANKER *like defendants awaiting sentence. Hoping for the best. Expecting a dose of knuckle.* WITHNAIL *composes himself.*

I don't know what my acquaintance did to upset you. But it was nothing to do with me . . .

Can WITHNAIL *really be saying this?* MARWOOD *is sweating adrenalin. His eyes are on the door. This has to be his only chance.*

I suggest you both go outside and discuss it sensibly in the
street . . .
Precisely where MARWOOD *is heading. But* WITHNAIL *is
through the door first. Bellowing.*
Get out of my way.
*He sprints into the street. For one who can hardly stand, he
moves at amazing speed. The solitary acid electric guitar gets
involved again. Bursts out with them . . .*

17. EXT. CAMDEN HIGH ROAD. DAY.
*And runs with them over this fast track. Two hundred yards are
covered at a hot foot.* WITHNAIL *slightly in the lead. They arrive
under the bridge and collapse gasping over railings.*
WITHNAIL: You could have grabbed the scarf. It was by your
   fucking feet . . .

18. INT. BATHROOM. APARTMENT. DAY.
*This bathroom is a psychological deterrent to cleanliness. It is
unclean. At some time in the past somebody has had an epileptic fit
in here with a can of fluorescent paint. There is wet rot and dry rot.
Evil-looking pustules are breaking through. A poster of Laurence
Olivier as Othello clings to one of the walls.*
MARWOOD (*V.O.*): Speed is like a dozen transatlantic flights
   without ever getting off the plane. Time change. You lose.
   You gain. Makes no difference so long as you keep taking
   the pills . . .
   *The room is very small. A lavatory at one end. A bath at the
   other. The type you sit up in like a huge enamel armchair.*
   MARWOOD *is sitting up in it. Pocked and shocked and
   attempting to shave. He wears a Shetland jumper rolled up to
   just under his armpits. This obviously affords protection
   against the cold. A mirror is propped behind the taps. His
   reflection appears in it.*
MARWOOD (*V.O.*): But some time or another you gotta get
   out. Because it's crashing. And all at once those frozen
   hours melt through the nervous system and seep out the
   pores.

He rinses the razor and shivers. WITHNAIL *bursts in wearing his overcoat.*

He clutches a couple of doses of fish and chips.

WITHNAIL: Bastards. Just to suck some miserable cheap cigar, and the bastards won't see me.

He thrusts a greasy parcel of newspaper across. MARWOOD *begins unwrapping it.* WITHNAIL *lowers the toilet seat and sits to eat.*

MARWOOD: Why are we having lunch in here?

WITHNAIL: It's dinner. And Danny's here.

MARWOOD: Danny? How'd he get in?

WITHNAIL: I let him in this morning. He's lost one of his clogs. He's come in because of this perpetual cold.

MARWOOD *seems concerned at the news. Produces an orange sausage.*

WITHNAIL: I hope tobacco sales plummet.

MARWOOD: I've got your saveloy.

WITHNAIL *stands. Pitches his fish and chips into the kazi and flushes it.*

I don't want it.

WITHNAIL: Then stick it in the soap tray and save it for later.

MARWOOD: Don't vent spleen on me. I'm in the same boat . . .

WITHNAIL: Stop *saying* that! You're not in the same boat! The only thing you're in that I've been in is this *fucking* bath. *He storms out muttering curses. Principally* 'They will suffer.' MARWOOD *lowers his chips. His eyes slip focus into the mirror.*

MARWOOD (*V.O. and playback*): Danny's here. Head-hunter to his friends. Head-hunter to everybody. He doesn't have any friends. The only people he converses with are his clients and occasionally the police. The purveyor of rare herbs and prescribed chemicals is back. Will we never be set free?

Focus continues to slip. Another face waits at the end of it.

19. INT. KITCHEN. APARTMENT. DAY.

DANNY *is a man who kept the* News of the World *in business all through the 1960s. And at the end of them put* Oz *out of it. He has dedicated his adult life to drugs. And it shows. He is a wreck. About sixty except he's twenty-six. A jade streak in his hair and night-black shades. Get down, punks. This man is before you were born.*

MARWOOD walks in wrapped in a towel. DANNY's voice is cultured Cockney. Monotoned. And brain-bummed.

DANNY: You're lookin' very beautiful man. Have you been away?

MARWOOD shakes his head. Fills the kettle and gives it the gas.

St Peter preached the epistles to the apostles looking like that. Have you got any food?

MARWOOD: I've got a saveloy.

The item is handed across. DANNY examines it as though it were some kind of deal. Gives it a sniffing and decides he likes it.

DANNY: How much is it?

MARWOOD: You can have it for nothing.

DANNY returns to the living room to put it in his bag.

WITHNAIL hobbles in re-togged in a tweed suit. It's old but has quality. Possibly came from a will. DANNY looks across with curiosity.

DANNY: I see you're wearin' a suit.

WITHNAIL: What's it gotta do with you?

One of WITHNAIL's boots is on the table. Matchsticks separate the sole from the uppers. A cobbling operation is in progress.

DANNY: No need to get uptight man. I was merely makin' an observation.

He slumps on the sofa. WITHNAIL carefully adjusts a paisley tie. I happened to be lookin' for a suit for the Coalman two weeks ago . . .

DANNY conducts an audit of the ashtray. Finds a suitable butt.

For reasons I can't really discuss with you, the Coalman had to go to Jamaica, and got busted comin' back through Heathrow . . .

WITHNAIL puts his boot on and stands on it to secure adhesion.

Had a weight under his Fez . . .

Half an inch of Gauloise is lit. WITHNAIL *pipes 'Make us a cup.'*

DANNY: We worked out it would be handykarma for him to get hold of a suit. But he's a very low temperature spade, the Coalman. Goes in in his kaftan and a bell . . .

The Gauloise produces a single cough before it takes a stubbing.

This doesn't go down at all well. They can handle the kaftan. They can't handle the bell. So there's this judge sittin' there in a cape like fuckin' Bat Man, with this re-ally rather far-out lookin' hat . . .

WITHNAIL: A wig.

DANNY: No man. This was more like a long white hat. And he looks at the Coalman and he says, what's all this? This is a court man, this ain't fancy-dress. So the Coalman looks at him, and he says, 'You think you look normal, your honour?' And the cunt gives him two years . . .

MARWOOD comes in with a couple of cups. Hands one to WITHNAIL.

I'm afraid I can't offer you gentlemen anything . . .

MARWOOD: That's all right, Danny. We decided to lay off for a bit.

DANNY: That's what I thought. 'Cept for personal use, I concur with you. As a mattera fact, I'm thinkina retirin' and goin' inta business.

WITHNAIL: Doing what?

DANNY: The toy industry.

WITHNAIL gestures to a small, pink child's hot-water bottle on the sofa. It's connected to straps and sprouts a yard of plastic pipe.

WITHNAIL: I thought you were in the bottle industry?
MARWOOD glances at the contraption and starts assembling clothes.
DANNY: No man. That's a sideline. You can have that. Instructions are included.
Nobody pays it any attention. WITHNAIL *decreases the pressure.*
Yeah, my partner's got an idea for makin' dolls. His name's Presuming Ed. His sister give him the idea. She got a doll on Christmas what pisses itself.
MARWOOD: Really?
DANNY: Yeah. Then you gotta change its drawers for it. S'horrible really, but they like that, the little girls. So we're gonna make one that shits itself as well . . .
WITHNAIL: Shits itself?
DANNY: He's an expert. He's buildin' the prototype now.
WITHNAIL decides to give his boot a test run. Makes a couple of journeys to the kitchen and back.
DANNY: Why is he behavin' so uptightly?
WITHNAIL: Because a gang of cheroot vendors considered a haircut beyond the limit of my abilities . . .
DANNY: I don't advise a haircut man. All hairdressers are in the employment of the government. Hairs are your aerials. They pick up signals from the cosmos, and transmit them directly into the brain. This is the reason bald-headed men are uptight.
WITHNAIL: What absolute twaddle.
WITHNAIL disguises glue with polish. MARWOOD *gets into a shirt.*
DANNY: Has he just been busted?
No he hasn't. MARWOOD *focuses into a mirror. Also wearing a tie.*
Then why's he wearin' that old suit?
WITHNAIL: Old suit? This suit was cut by Hawke's of Savile Row. Just because the best tailoring you've ever seen is above your fucking appendix doesn't mean anything.
DANNY: Don't get uptight with me man. 'Cause, if you do, I'll

have to give you a dose of medicine. And if I spike you, you'll know you've been spoken to.

WITHNAIL: You wouldn't spike me. You're too mean. Anyway, there's nothing invented I couldn't take.

This is dangerous talk. MARWOOD *is beginning to look concerned.*

DANNY: If I medicined you, you'd think a brain tumour was a birthday present.

WITHNAIL: I could take *double* anything you could.

There is a very long pause. The apothecary rolls a tongue over his contaminated teeth. Takes his glasses off and somehow manages to lower an eye in his head. He may be smiling. If Fritz Lang were alive he'd be a star.

DANNY: Very, very foolish words man.

There's a confrontation coming. MARWOOD *moves in to defuse it.*

MARWOOD: He's right, Withnail. Don't be a fool. Look at him, his mechanism's gone. He's taken more drugs than you've had hot dinners.

WITHNAIL: I'm not having this shag-sack insulting me. Let him get his drugs out . . .

WITHNAIL *watches with a supercilious leer as* DANNY *empties his shopping bag. Horrible things in it. Food remains. Dead flowers. A bottle of nail varnish. And a rubber doll. Perhaps the prototype? He holds it menacingly at* WITHNAIL.

DANNY: This doll is extremely dangerous. It has voodoo qualities.

WITHNAIL *sniggers at it. Enrages its owner. Its bald and ugly little head is torn off and its guts emptied on to the table. Two dozen coloured spansules. A dozen soiled and assorted pills.* DANNY *sifts through isolating a tiny pink tablet. He looks up at* WITHNAIL *as though this item prevents all further argument.*

DANNY: Trade – phenodihydrochloride – benzorex. Street – the embalmer.

WITHNAIL: Balls. I'll swallow it and run a mile.

WITHNAIL *reaches for it. A khaki finger detains it where it is.*

DANNY: Cool your boots man. This pill's valued at two quid.

WITHNAIL: Two quid? You're outa your mind.

MARWOOD: That's sense, Withnail.

WITHNAIL: You can stick it up your arse for nothing, and fuck off while you're doing it.

DANNY: No need to insult me man. I was leavin' anyway.

He gathers his equipment and stands. Slings a pelt around him.

Have either of you got shoes?

20. EXT. CHELSEA EMBANKMENT. EVENING.
Moisture puts the city out of focus. The Jaguar speeds along the Embankment. One headlight is functioning on the driver's side, one windscreen wiper on the passenger's. The car turns into a crescent of imposing Victorian houses. Pulls up and the pair of them get out.

WITHNAIL *checks his sole before crossing the road.*

MARWOOD *follows straightening his trousers. Parked opposite is a huge Sedanca Rolls. 1948 and immaculate.* WITHNAIL *looks approvingly as they pass. This is 'Monty's car'.*

21. INT. HALLWAY/CHELSEA HOUSE. EVENING.
A brass lion's head knocker goes into operation. Here's a sight. A wall of Mozart with UNCLE MONTY *standing in front of it. He holds a cat in his right hand and a glass teapot filled with water in his left. He's delighted to see them. With a rococo sweep of the dangling cat he ushers them in and the coats come off.* MONTY *is large with a reptilian quality. His nose dominates the face and is the colour of port. Somehow his head has managed to grow round his glasses like trees grow round wire. In his lapel is a radish the same colour as his nose.*

MONTY: Sit down. Do. Would you like a drink?

MARWOOD *puts in for a gin and tonic and* WITHNAIL *for a sherry.* WITHNAIL *is obviously to be taken seriously. There's a trolley full of malt whisky here so he is out to make a good impression. Paintings and tapestries decorate the walls.*

MARWOOD is somewhat uncomfortable in these surroundings. In complete contrast WITHNAIL *is totally at ease. Apart from the magnificent furniture the room is filled with vegetables. Cauliflowers and carrots are on every surface in valuable antique pots. A silver tray on the table sprouts a dozen fully grown onions. In the bay window is a fucking great cabbage the size of an aspidistra.* MARWOOD *is staring at its luxurious foliage when* UNCLE MONTY *pirouettes in with the drinks.*

MONTY: Do you like vegetables?

MARWOOD nods and MONTY *wafts dust from the leaves of a parsnip.*

I've always been fond of root crops, but I only started to grow last summer . . .

MONTY proffers glasses and WITHNAIL *moves in for a* 'Chin chin'.

I happen to think the cauliflower more beautiful than the rose.

He moves off at speed towards a turnip in an art nouveau *pot.*

Do you grow?

WITHNAIL: Geraniums . . .

News to MARWOOD. MONTY *swings towards him. Exchange of smiles.*

MONTY: You little traitors. I think the carrot infinitely more fascinating than the geranium. The carrot has mystery. Flowers are essentially tarts. Prostitutes for the bees . . .

All this is said isolating MARWOOD. *He returns an uneasy smile.* MONTY *evaporates into the kitchen with a giggle towards* WITHNAIL.

Help yourselves to another drink.

WITHNAIL *immediately leaps to his feet and downs several huge gulps of whisky from the bottle. Corks it quickly and refills his glass with more sherry.* MARWOOD *is whispering in concern.*

MARWOOD: What's all this? The man's mad.

WITHNAIL: Eccentric.

MARWOOD: Eccentric? He's insane. Not only that, he's a raving homosexual . . .

They reseat at speed and attempt to look relaxed. The cat comes skidding out, followed by MONTY *with a purple face. He lumbers after it with veins throbbing.*

MONTY: Beastly little parasite. How dare you? You little thug. How dare you?

A degree of surprise from the assembled as MONTY *goes after the mog. It shelters behind a leek and he concedes to its agility. Wiping sweat from his brow* MONTY *calms and sits next to* MARWOOD.

MONTY: Beastly ungrateful little swine . . .

WITHNAIL: Shall I get you a drink, Monty?

A crimson silk handkerchief returns to MONTY's *breast pocket.*

MONTY: Yes, yes, yes please dear boy. You can prepare me a small rhesus-negative Bloody Mary. And you must tell me all the news. I haven't seen you since you finished the last film . . .

And MARWOOD's *certain he hasn't seen the first either.*

WITHNAIL: Rather busy, Uncle . . . TV and stuff. And my agent's attempting to edge me towards the Royal Shakespeare Company again.

MONTY: Splendid.

WITHNAIL: And he's just had an audition for rep.

MONTY: Oh splendid. So you're a thesbian too?

MARWOOD *is not a little taken aback by the word 'thesbian'.*

WITHNAIL: Monty used to act.

MONTY: Oh, I'd hardly say that. It's true I crept the boards in my youth. But I never really had it in my blood . . . and that's what's so essential, isn't it? Theatrical zeal in the veins? Alas, I have little more than vintage wine and memories.

And one of them is on the crowded mantelpiece. A photograph of Monty in his youth. A sepia reminiscence in a doublet and hose. He stands and almost clasps it. A dose of mothballs and Adelphi.

It is the most shattering experience of a young man's life,

when one morning he awakes, and quite reasonably says to himself, I will *never* play the Dane. When that moment comes, one's ambition ceases . . .

He turns back towards MARWOOD, *his voice sonorous with emotion.*

Don't you agree?

WITHNAIL: It's a part I intend to play, Uncle.

MONTY: And you'd be *marvellous* . . . marvellous . . .

MONTY is suddenly on the ramparts. Whispering at the Ghost he never saw. Now located somewhere towards the ceiling of the apartment. MARWOOD has had enough of this. Moves on WITHNAIL with a whisper.

MARWOOD: Let's get out of here . . . come on. He's a madman. Any minute now he's gonna rush out and get into his tights.

WITHNAIL: O K. OK. Gimme a minute.

MARWOOD: The house, or out.

WITHNAIL is persuaded and approaches MONTY who turns dew-eyed.

WITHNAIL: Could I have a word with you Monty?

MONTY: Forgive me, forgive me. I was allowing memory to have the better of me. Seeing you boys, so young, so filled with the fire of the theatre, puts a sting of nostalgia into one's nose . . .

WITHNAIL agrees and manoeuvres him to the sofa. MARWOOD wanders into the Mozart as WITHNAIL hits the old bastard with a sherry. Too much music and too far away to hear what is said. But WITHNAIL is in full-throated ease. MARWOOD examines a table infected with silver-framed photographs. One of a little boy sitting on the running board of a vintage Bentley. Monty is at the wheel. The little boy in the straw hat is clearly Withnail. WITHNAIL is suddenly on his feet and heading for the drinks. He shoots a glance at MARWOOD. Evidently pulled it off. The house is in the bag. MARWOOD is delighted and drifts back into the conversation.

MONTY: Indeed, I remember my first agent. Raymond Duck.

Withnail (Richard E. Grant) and I (Paul McGann) on their rejuvenating holiday.

Withnail persuades Uncle Monty (Richard Griffiths) to loan him his country cottage.

He was a dreadful little Israelite. Four floors up on the Charing Cross Road and never a job at the top of them . . .

WITHNAIL *is pouring whisky. Confident he has landed his fish.* MONTY *redirects eyes to a hovering* MARWOOD.

I'm told you are a writer too.

MARWOOD *can't find any reaction here but a shrug and a smile.*

Do you write poems?

MARWOOD: No, I wish I could. Just thoughts, really.

MONTY: Are you published?

MARWOOD: Oh no.

MONTY: Where did you school?

WITHNAIL *takes a sudden interest in the conversation and says:*

WITHNAIL: He went to the other place, Monty.

MARWOOD *doesn't know what the 'other place' is.* MONTY *does and is launching into a sentence beginning, 'Oh, you went to Eton . . .' when something terrible happens. At this most crucial stage in the negotiations the cat reappears. For reasons best known to itself it throws itself at* WITHNAIL. MONTY *rears to his feet driving the already dangerous levels of blood pressure into the capillaries of his swollen conk.*

MONTY: Get that damned little swine out of here. It's trying to get itself in with you. Trying for even more advantage. It's obsessed with its gut. It's like a bloody rugby ball now.

Swinging his arms wildly he makes towards WITHNAIL *and his cat in a menacing stoop. Both manage to get out of his way. Snorting oaths the uncle follows the animal to a corner where it snarls in horror.* MONTY *swivels seeking to cut off escape.* MARWOOD *and* WITHNAIL *watch in amazement as pursuit continues.* MONTY *lumbers through his tray of onions and the cat suddenly vanishes.*

It will die. It will die.

WITHNAIL *takes his arm and manages to escort him to the sofa.*

WITHNAIL: Let me get you a top up . . .
Ill-charted maps of the Orinoco delta throb in MONTY's
temples.
MONTY: No, dear boy, you must leave, you must leave. Yet
again that oaf has destroyed my day.
Everything is slipping away. MARWOOD *doesn't seem to care
any more. Despite all work put in with this raving aberration
he is prepared to leave instantly. So it seems is* WITHNAIL.
Then a thought. And a change of gear.
WITHNAIL: Listen, Monty, could I just have a quick word
with you in private? -
MONTY *looks at him, preparing to say no. But* WITHNAIL *is
earnest. Groaning 'Very well,' he allows himself to be shunted
towards a bedroom.* MARWOOD *has no idea what the plan is.
But even so isn't entirely happy with it. He stares after them
till the door shuts.*
*On the instant the cat reappears displaying the stealth that
secures its existence in such uncongenial lodgings.* MARWOOD
*eyes it with vague animosity. But the thing is no longer of
importance. Finishing his whisky he finds himself back at the
windows. Night and lights and mist on the river.*
Any more of this and it's art.
MARWOOD (*V.O.*): How many more maniacs out there?
Nurturing their turnips. Living in greenhouses with
paranoid cats terrified by the sonnets of the Bard?
Possibly thousands. Those with the money are eccentric.
Those without. Insane.
The door suddenly opens. MONTY *out first. Considerably
mellowed and showing stabilisation of blood pressure.*
WITHNAIL *out next. Doesn't meet* MARWOOD's *eyes but
walks straight into the hall for his coat.* MARWOOD *swaps a
smile with* MONTY *and they vanish into an entrance hall.*

22. INT. ENTRANCE HALL. HOUSE. NIGHT.
A huge red-pepper plant and a bust of a boy. MARWOOD *is glad to
be out but vaguely ill at ease.*
MARWOOD: Whass all this going off in private business?

33

WITHNAIL *answers with an enigmatic and annoying smile.*
Why'd you tell him I went to Eton?
WITHNAIL: Because it wouldn't have helped if I hadn't. I was
just trying to establish you in some sort of context he'd
understand . . .
MARWOOD: What d'you mean by that?
The elevator arrives and WITHNAIL *leads the way in. A
smug smile on his kisser a large iron key dangling from his
finger.*
WITHNAIL: I mean, *free* to those that can afford it, *very
expensive* to those that can't.

23. INT. SERVICE PIT. GARAGE. DAY.
*A greasy little back-street dungeon. The Jaguar is shoulder height
on a hydraulic jack.* WITHNAIL *and* MARWOOD *watch while a
weaselish* MECHANIC *pokes beneath it with a naked 100-watt
bulb in a little wire cage. Doesn't like the look of what he sees.
Stubbing his butt he emerges to address* MARWOOD.
MECHANIC: Bob or two either sida forty quid.
MARWOOD: Forty quid? If we had forty quid, we'd buy a
better car.
MECHANIC: This thing's unroadworthy. I've seen better tyres
hanging over the side of a tug.
WITHNAIL: Nonsense. It's in first-class condition. Right, get
it down, we'll service it ourselves.

24. EXT. GARAGE FORECOURT. DAY.
*And the shot cranes down. Music and a bit of drizzle about. The
Jag rumbles in and they dismount.* WITHNAIL *opens the boot,
shouting mechanical instructions at* MARWOOD.
WITHNAIL: Right, you service the water and I'll service the
tyres. Then you can service the battery, and then we'll go
home and get under the sink.
*An air hose and a watering can. A free service and a slow
dissolve which the music survives.*

25. INT. KITCHEN. APARTMENT. DAY.

WITHNAIL *is arse out on his knees in the cupboard under the sink.*
A forest of bottles surrounds him. Regiments of Guinness and Bass.
MARWOOD *is computing their value with a pad and pencil. The*
last bottle comes out and WITHNAIL *stands and prepares for the*
total.

MARWOOD: I make it a tanner under four quid.

WITHNAIL: All right, let's work this out. Three pounds
nineteen and six, plus thirteen pounds three and nine
National Assistance, plus your thirty-two quid three and
four, that makes fifty pounds six and seven.

MARWOOD: Does it?

WITHNAIL: I've just said so, haven't I. Right, at eight and
eleven a bottle, that means we can have ninety-six bottles
of Greek Hock.

MARWOOD: Ninety-six bottles of Greek Hock? You're out of
your fucking mind.

WITHNAIL *starts loading the empties.* MARWOOD *counts the*
money.

WITHNAIL: I'm not suggesting we spend the entire amount on
Greek Hock. We'll have nine two-and-a-half litres of
Eye-tie red and three dozen barley wines . . .

MARWOOD: How much is that?

26. INT. OFF LICENCE. DAY.

A horrible pinstripe suit. Dandruff. This is their wine BROKER.
And they're broke. And this is his wine. And WITHNAIL*'s pissed.*

BROKER: Fifteen pounds twelve and a penny.

WITHNAIL: Good. We'll have a bottle of Haig.

The BROKER *goes about it.* MARWOOD *is unhappy with the*
last item.

MARWOOD: Don't be an idiot. We can't afford it.

The whisky joins the wine. The BROKER *observes without*
comment.

WITHNAIL: You've had petrol. I want whisky.

MARWOOD: *I've* had petrol? We've *both* had petrol.

WITHNAIL: You've had *oil.*

MARWOOD: *Of course* I've had oil! It's four hundred miles . . .
WITHNAIL: I'm not sitting in that wreck all night without
    whisky. It's essential.
    *He moves for the bottle – arm on same plane as the wrecking
    ball.*

27. EXT. DEMOLITION SITE/STREET. CAMDEN TOWN. DAY.

*Mr Hendrix plays Mr Dylan's 'All Along the Watch Tower'. This
music will choreograph the journey north. The music starts here.
Violence on electric guitar. Violence in the street. That fucking
great demolition ball is in action. Puts one into the belly of a wall
and it collapses like a drunk. Much rubble and dust. As it draws
back for another blow the camera moves with it and keeps moving
on to the Jag.* WITHNAIL *already inside with his bottle of whisky.*
MARWOOD *gets into the driving seat. He wears clip-on shades on
his glasses. He starts the car and glances across at the site. With one
finger he flicks the shades down. The car disappears under the
bridge.*

28. EXT. STREET. SUBURBS. LONDON. DAY.

*The music heads north with the Jaguar through the wastelands of
Finchley and Hendon. A scrag land of TV aerials and faces in
corporate shock. Miles and miles of recently constructed high-rise
slums. Each with its architecturally designed and resident-
vandalised tree.*

    *A roar from the twin punctured exhausts. They pass a line of
schoolgirls at a bus stop.* WITHNAIL *hanging from his window.*
WITHNAIL: *Scrubbers. Scrubbers.*

29. INT. JAG SEDAN. DAY.

WITHNAIL *clasps the Haig. Laughing out and pissed as a gorilla.*
MARWOOD: Shut up . . .
WITHNAIL: Little tarts. They love it . . .
MARWOOD: Listen to me. I'm trying to drive this thing as
    quietly as possible. If you don't shut up, we're gonna get
    stopped by the police. Gimme the bottle.

MARWOOD *grabs the whisky. Takes a hit.* WITHNAIL *grabs it back. Another guzzle at the bottle. And another exterior attraction. They pass a sign:* 'ACCIDENT BLACK SPOT. DRIVE WITH EXTREME CARE. LONDON BOROUGH OF FINCHLEY.'

WITHNAIL: Look at that! Look at that! Accident black spot! These aren't *accidents.* They're *throwing themselves into the road!* Gladly! Throwing themselves into the road to escape all this hideousness.

A yob on a corner. The window goes down again.

WITHNAIL *screams.*

Throw yourself into the road, darling. You haven't got a chance.

The car vanishes into a perspective of street and exhaust fumes.

30. EXT. MI. MOTORWAY ENTRANCE RAMP. DAY.
The Jag is giving its ninety. Brutal rust on a traffic-free road.

31. EXT. MI. MOTORWAY. EVENING.
Factories and power stations and morbid industrial complexes. The land is in ruins and so is the sky. Great greasy clouds are piling on the horizon. It'll be dark in less than an hour.

WITHNAIL (*V.O.*): At some time or another, I wanna stop and get hold of a child . . .

MARWOOD (*V.O.*): What d'you want a child for?

WITHNAIL (*V.O.*): To tutor it in the ways of righteousness, and procure some uncontaminated urine.

32. INT. JAGUAR SEDAN. EVENING.
WITHNAIL *is unravelling plastic hose from the hot-water bottle. Trying to work out where the strings and straps should be. Gets the bottle under an armpit and starts waving some sort of valve.*

WITHNAIL: This is a device enabling the drunken driver to operate in absolute safety. You fill it with piss, take this pipe down the trouser, and Sellotape this valve to the end of the old chap. Then you get horribly drunk, and they can't fucking touch you.

MARWOOD *glances across. An instruction sheet takes an unfolding.*

WITHNAIL: According to these instructions, you refuse everything but a urine sample. You undo your valve, give 'em a dose of unadulterated child's piss, and they have to give you your keys back.

WITHNAIL *takes another large slug of whisky. So does* MARWOOD.

WITHNAIL: Danny's a genius. I'm gonna have a doze.

33. EXT. MI. MOTORWAY. EVENING.
Bridges and other roadside bollocks. The Jaguar thunders past.

34. EXT. MOTORWAY INTERSECTION. DEEP EVENING.
A scraping of daylight left. Headlight on the Jag swings off the motorway on to a minor road. Going to piss down any minute now.

35. EXT. COUNTRY ROAD. VALLEY. DEEPER EVENING.
The Jaguar hits the rain. Hardly any decrease in speed. Black and ominous-looking hills. Balls of black cloud rolling into a valley. The car descends with them. The brake lights come on, and the music ends.

36. EXT. COUNTRY ROAD. NIGHT.
MARWOOD *pulls over and climbs out. One hell of a gale is blowing. He gets to the passenger side of the car. Starts wrenching at the still-moving wiper blade.* WITHNAIL's *face is periodically visible. Wrecked in his seat and asleep with his jaw wide open.* MARWOOD *fails to relocate the wiper blade. Soaking wet and furious he staggers back to his door. Slams it with nothing achieved.*

37. INT. JAGUAR SEDAN. NIGHT.
The force of MARWOOD's *entry wakes his co-pilot and navigator. Nothing but the beat of the windscreen wiper.*

WITHNAIL: Are we there?

MARWOOD: No we're not. We're here. And we're in the middle of a fucking gale.

He starts the engine and pulls out. Snaps instructions at
WITHNAIL.
You'll have to keep a lookout your side. If you see anything, tell me. And get holda that map.
WITHNAIL *emits an accelerating groan. Something to do with a headache. He looks across. Eyes like a pair of decayed clams.*

WITHNAIL: Where's the whisky?

MARWOOD: What for?

WITHNAIL: I got a bastard behind the eyes. I can't take aspirins without a drink . . .
The bottle is discovered. The cork popped. And back to
MARWOOD.
Where's the aspirins?

MARWOOD: Probably in the bathroom.

WITHNAIL: You mean we've come out here in the middle of fucking nowhere without aspirins?
This appears to be the case. WITHNAIL *is becoming emotional.*

MARWOOD: Where are we?

WITHNAIL: How should I know where we are? I feel like a pig shat in my head.

MARWOOD: Get hold of that map, and look for a place called Crow Crag.

WITHNAIL: I can't. I've gone blind. My bladder's exploding. I've got to have a slash.

MARWOOD: You can't have one.
MARWOOD *is nearly in* WITHNAIL's *lap trying to see some road.*

WITHNAIL: What do you mean I *can't* have one? I've *got* to have one. Stop this bastard and let me out.

MARWOOD: No. Look at the map. Find a biro cross.
WITHNAIL *grabs it. Practically destroys it. Approaches a shout.*

WITHNAIL: We're about a *yard* from London, and going up a hill! Now, for Christ's sake, stop this crate and let me out.

38. EXT. COUNTRY ROAD. NIGHT.

The night is overpoweringly black. Towards the end of his monumentally long piss WITHNAIL *turns to* MARWOOD.

WITHNAIL: I think all this is a mistake. A serious and soon-to-be-regretted mistake.

39. EXT. COUNTRYSIDE. NIGHT.

The Jag winds up a maze of stone walls.

The Jag passes a concealed entrance. Backs up to reveal a sign saying Crow Crag Farm. Takes this turning.

The car passes through Crow Crag Farm and continues.

The Jaguar bumps down a rutted track in deep night.

WITHNAIL's *P.O.V. interior car. Windscreen wiper battling the rain. A house comes into view.*

Above the car as its single headlight sweeps a bleak-looking cottage.

At a glance picturesque. Mud conspires to prevent MARWOOD's *sharp right-angled turn into the yard. The car slides into the gate. A crank of a handbrake and they get out.*

WITHNAIL: There must and shall be aspirin . . .

MARWOOD *levers a pair of suitcases and grocery bags from the car. Violent rain sweeps through the single headlight.*

WITHNAIL *hangs over the partially open gate like laundry.*

If I don't get aspirin, I shall die, here, on this fucking mountainside.

Staggers, groaning, to the front door and gets pushed aside.

MARWOOD: Give me the key. And get outta the way.

40. INT. COTTAGE. NIGHT.

The door opens, revealing a smudge of headlight from outside.

MARWOOD *strikes a match and* WITHNAIL *whispers,* 'Christ Almighty.' *In the instant before the match goes out they see crumbling walls and stale shadows and giant atlases of damp on the floor. They also see an oil lamp. The match goes out. Another one is lit. A yellow glow and the lamp reveals all. Table with several chairs. Old but not antique. A photograph of a football team. All with moustaches and shorts down to their knees. 'Oxford 1926.' Is*

*one of them Monty? Two armchairs and a chaise-longue with
stuffing hanging out. A grate.* MARWOOD *journeys into an
adjoining room. Checks stairs and turns back to a sink with a rusty
pump. He drags the lever down. A rheumatic whine. No water.
The wind howls like wolves. He moves back into the kitchen and
discovers* WITHNAIL *sitting in a chair.*

MARWOOD: What are you doing?

A pair of shocked and horn-rimmed eyes focus in his direction.

WITHNAIL: Sitting down to enjoy my holiday.

Blasts of icy intensity rocket down the chimney. WITHNAIL
could be standing on a cliff. MARWOOD *checks out a huge
range and turns back to* WITHNAIL *forcing the optimism.*

MARWOOD: All right, we're gonna have to approach this
scientifically. First thing is to get a fire alight. Then we'll
split into two fact-finding groups. I'll deal with the water
and other plumbings. You can check the fuel and wood
situation.

41. INT. LIVING ROOM. COTTAGE. NIGHT.

*With an abundance of acrid smoke a minute fire smoulders in the
grate.* MARWOOD *dumps blankets and goes for the pump. Cranks
violently. A dozen strokes and a flood of khaki water erupts.
Euphoria.* WITHNAIL *barges through the front door in time to
observe this phenomenon. Wet and gale-blasted and carrying a
twig.*

MARWOOD: What's that?

WITHNAIL: The fuel and wood situation. There's fuck all out
there except a hurricane.

*The fuel and wood situation gets thrown on the fire. One or
two burnt-out logs in the grate.* MARWOOD *puts them on and
joins* WITHNAIL *in the opposite chair. They stare into the
fire. At every change of the wind they are engulfed in smoke.
This place is uninhabitable.*

MARWOOD: Give it a chance. It's gotta warm up.

WITHNAIL: *Warm up?* We may as well sit round a cigarette.

MARWOOD *takes a large slug of whisky. Hands the bottle
across.* WITHNAIL *practically finishes it. Lights a cigarette*

*and starts coughing as he's temporarily obscured by another
dose of smoke.*

This is ridiculous. We'll be found dead in here next
spring. I've got a blinding, fucking headache. I must have
heat.

*So saying he rises to his pins and demolishes the nearest chair.
Flames suddenly appear.* WITHNAIL *assaults another and
the room shifts through a speedy dissolve.*

42. INT. (ANOTHER ANGLE). LIVING ROOM. COTTAGE.
NIGHT.

*The room is filled with smoke. Only cigarette ends are visible. Both
squat in their overcoats in front of a cold fire.* WITHNAIL *slings
another chair leg on.*

WITHNAIL: Whatever happens we've got to keep this bastard
   burning.

   *There's a door banging outside. The wind is devouring the
   house.*

MARWOOD: We've got enough furniture for tonight. We'll get
   down that farm tomorrow and get logs.

WITHNAIL: All this is a mistake. I tell you. This is a dreadful
   mistake.

43. INT. BEDROOM. COTTAGE. DAY.

MARWOOD *wears his overcoat like a dressing gown. Boots like
slippers. Wind still hammers the house. He looks out of his window.
The rain has stopped. Little view except the side of a shed.
Grabbing his clothes he shambles into* WITHNAIL's *room. Its
occupant is heaped under blankets and overcoat and asleep.
Decides not to wake him and quietly closes the door and heads
downstairs.*

44. INT. HALL/BOUDOIR. COTTAGE. DAY.

*A tub full of walking sticks at the bottom of the stairs. Plus a hat
rack featuring a couple of country-type caps and a fencing mask.*
MARWOOD *notices an épée in the tub. He's about to walk out of
the door when he decides to explore a room he missed last night . . .*

opens the door on to a Victorian-looking room. A 1930s record
player with a stack of records. Dismal early Georgian furniture.
Most of the chairs and paintings are decorated with dribbles of bird
shit. He notices a dead (down the chimney) crow, before shutting
the door and walking across the little outside yard.

45. EXT. COURTYARD. COTTAGE. DAY.
MARWOOD *opens a wood–gate and walks down a short entrance of*
brick. Fumbles for his glasses and puts them on. And here it is!
Here is a fifteen-mile-long picture postcard. Bleak but beautiful. A
lake stretches away to the left furnished with pines. Optimism cuts
in as he heads back to the house.

46. EXT. TRACK. HILLSIDE OVER FARM. DAY.
MARWOOD *is fully dressed and filled with a slow puncture of*
enthusiasm. He carries a walking stick and wears a cheese-cutter
cap. But the country image doesn't last long. It dissolves with every
step. Midway between the cottage and the farmhouse his boots are
saturated. Cows turn to see him pass. He comes to a halt at a gate.
SHUT THIS GATE. *A few yards past it and he sees why. Twenty*
feet in front of him is a big bull with horns on its head. Neither of
them likes the look of the other and MARWOOD *climbs a wall. No*
more path. This is virtually wading. At a safe distance he reclimbs
the wall. Continues towards the farmhouse. The wind practically
takes his glasses off. Angry black clouds massing.

47. EXT. CROW CRAG FARMHOUSE. DAY.
A large and mysterious-looking building constructed of local stone.
Curtains drawn and looks deserted. MARWOOD *comes in over a*
fence and walks towards it. Clears mud from his boots. An
imposing front door. It takes a knockering. No response and
another knock. Sounds of footsteps over stone.
VOICE (*O.S.*): Who's there?
MARWOOD: Me.
> *The door opens. Here's an* OLD BIRD *in an apron and*
> *hobnailed boots.*
OLD BIRD: What do you want?

MARWOOD *stares at her. She stares back. She's horrible and seventy and suspicious. Is this the crow that made the farm famous?*

MARWOOD: I'm a friend of Montague Withnail. He's lent us his cottage.

She freezes a hard so what? MARWOOD *tries to smile at her. Fails.*

I wondered if you could sell us some food? Eggs and things?

OLD CROW: No. We ain't a shop.

MARWOOD: What about wood and coal?

OLD CROW: No.

Maybe it's his accent she doesn't like. He tries another tack.

MARWOOD: I'm not from London, you know.

HORRIBLE OLD CROW: I don't care where you come from.

And MARWOOD *gets a faceful of door. He stares at it a moment. Turns away. Walks fifteen feet backwards and looks at penned sheep. Looks at the house.*

MARWOOD (V.O.): Not the attitude I'd been given to expect from the H. E. Bates novel I'd read. I thought they'd all be out the back drinking cider and discussing butter. Clearly a myth.

He decides to have another go. Back to the door. Another knock. It starts to rain.

Evidently country people are no more receptive to strangers than city dwellers.

The footsteps return. But this time she declines to open up.

MARWOOD: D'you think you could tell me where I could buy some coal and wood?

OLD CROW (O.S.): You'll have to see my son. He runs this farm.

MARWOOD: Where is your son?

OLD CROW (O.S.): Up in top fields. You can't miss him. His leg's bound in polythene.

48. EXT. HILL OVER HOUSE/STREAM/COURTYARD. DAY.
MARWOOD *comes over the hill. Obviously slipped in shit more*

*times than I care to detail. Angry and soaked to the skin, he pounds
into the courtyard and disappears into the house.*

49. INT. KITCHEN. COTTAGE. DAY.
Rain beats the window. MARWOOD *beats the ceiling with a
saucepan.*

MARWOOD: Wake up, you bastard. You have to get wood.
*He works the pump. Washes himself with spurts of icy water.
Finds time to continue bashing the ceiling with his pan.*
Wake up! Wake up, you bastard!
*A gale blows through the house. Without a fire the chimney is
like having a hole in the roof.* WITHNAIL *shuffles in wearing
his overcoat. Catches a hostile glare as* MARWOOD *heads for
the hearth and sits to wrench his boots off.*

WITHNAIL: Jesus – you're covered in shit.

MARWOOD: I tried to get fuel and wood. There's a miserable
little pensioner down there. She wouldn't give it
to me.

WITHNAIL: Where are we gonna get it then?

MARWOOD: There's a man up the mountain. Why he's up
there, fuck knows. But he's up there with a leg bound in
polythene. You can't miss him. He's the man.
MARWOOD *succeeds in removing his boots. Takes a slug of
whisky.*

MARWOOD: Have another look in that shed. Find anything.
And if you can't find anything, bring in the shed.

50. INT. LIVING ROOM. COTTAGE. DAY.
*Another dining chair has gone on. The room is again filled with
smoke. They sit on either side of the fire eating breakfast.
Unsuitable foods under the circumstances. Plastic carrier bags
produce an apple. A camembert. Whisky and wine.* MARWOOD
cuts an apple in half and offers it to WITHNAIL. *He refuses and
lights a cigarette.*

MARWOOD: How come Monty owns such a horrible little
shack?

WITHNAIL: I've no idea.

And he stands and starts pacing and the wind howls outside.

MARWOOD: Never discuss your family, do you?

WITHNAIL: I fail to see my family is of any interest to you – I have absolutely no interest in yours – I dislike relatives in general, and my own in particular.

MARWOOD: Why?

WITHNAIL discovers an épée in the stick bin and fences the air.

WITHNAIL: Because . . . I've told you why . . . we're incompatible. They don't like me being on stage.

MARWOOD: Then they must be delighted with your career.

WITHNAIL: What d'you mean?

MARWOOD: You rarely are.

MARWOOD's cynicism inspires Shakespearian activity with the épée.

WITHNAIL: You just wait. Just you wait. When I strike, they won't know what hit 'em.

A very low rumble a long way away. They hear it simultaneously and it takes WITHNAIL to the door.

There's a tractor approaching.

MARWOOD instantly animates. Begins shoving feet into his boots.

MARWOOD: Get after him. That must be the man.

51. EXT. COTTAGE. GARDENS/TRACK. DAY.

WITHNAIL *is attempting to cross a potato patch without damaging his boots. Bellowing* 'Get out of the way' MARWOOD *barges past. The wind takes their breath and voices away.* WITHNAIL *mounts the wall and stands on top of it, waving like a nancy sailor. This has zero affect on the tractor. It's passing at speed about forty yards away. Abandoning all regard for personal wellbeing* MARWOOD *clambers the wall and races through the mud waving his arms like a maniac. Finally manages to attract the driver's attention. He stops and they descend on him.*

A face looks out of the cab. Registers alarm at the fury of these idiots' approach. WITHNAIL *grabs at a mudguard as if to stop the tractor getting away. Shouts up at the staring* FARMER.

WITHNAIL: Are you the farmer?

There is a reticence in ISACS PARKIN *to speak with these two.*

MARWOOD: Shut up. I'll deal with this.

MARWOOD *takes control and* ISACS PARKIN *shuts his engine down.*

WITHNAIL: We've gone on holiday by mistake. We're in this cottage here.

ISACS PARKIN *looks down at this shit-streaked wreck in surprise.*

Are you the farmer?

MARWOOD: Stop saying that, Withnail. Of course he's the fucking farmer.

The farmer can't hear. Opens his door. A leg bound in polythene. Also a plaster cast. The polythene is evidently to keep out damp.

We're friends of Montague Withnail. We desperately need fuel and wood.

An exchange of eyes. PARKIN *stares. Repeats* 'Montague Withnail?'

Montague Withnail. You must know him. He's a fat man. He owns the cottage.

ISACS PARKIN: I seen a fat man. Lunnon type. Queer sort. But his name's French or summit.

WITHNAIL: French?

ISACS PARKIN: Adrienne de la Touche. But he ain't been here for a coupla years. Last time I seen him was with his son.

Even under these circumstances, MARWOOD *finds a sort of a smile.*

MARWOOD: That's him.

WITHNAIL: Listen, we're bona fide. We don't come from London. Can we have some fuel and wood?

ISACS PARKIN: I could bring you some logs up later. I gotta feed the cows and that first.

WITHNAIL: When?

MARWOOD: Shut up. That would be very nice of you. What

47

about food? D'you think you could sell us something to
eat?

ISACS PARKIN: I could bring you a chicken. But you'll have to
go into the village really.

MARWOOD: That would be very kind of you.

PARKIN *swings his stiffened leg inside and starts the engine.*
What happened to your leg?

ISACS PARKIN: Got a randy bull down there. Give us one in
the knee.

*He guns the engine and vanishes down the track. Smiles
emerge. They head back to the cottage with a sense of
achievement. It's going to get better. And Al Bowley is
already beginning to play.*

52. INT. LIVING ROOM. COTTAGE. DAY.

*A record continues to scrape. But things are looking up in here.
Logs are coming. And they have made free with the furniture.*
WITHNAIL's *almost whistling as he goes about his duties at the
grate. He's invented some sort of draught deflector out of a sheet of
iron. It is moderately successful in directing smoke up the chimney.
He opens the oven door and shoves his boots in. Closes the door as*
MARWOOD *appears from the kitchen. The latter removes a
cauldron of boiling water from the fire.*

MARWOOD: You wanna get out the back, don't you? Get some
spuds up?

WITHNAIL *doesn't like the idea. Has a perfect excuse.*

WITHNAIL: Sorry, I can't. My boots are in the oven.

MARWOOD: You'd go out if you had boots?

WITHNAIL: Gladly.

MARWOOD *stands and walks into the kitchen. Reappears
instantly.* WITHNAIL *looks suspiciously at a pair of plastic
carrier bags.*

MARWOOD: We can tie 'em up with string.

53. EXT. GARDEN. COTTAGE. DAY.

WITHNAIL *emerges from the front door wearing his overcoat and a
pair of carrier bags. He clasps a carving fork and heads for the*

potato patch. MARWOOD *stands at the door. Shouts directions concerning the location of the potato. The fork goes in and a fibrous little marble comes out.* 'I've got one. I've got one.'

54. EXT. COURTYARD. COTTAGE. NIGHT.

The camera stares in the window. WITHNAIL *asleep in front of the fire.* MARWOOD *at the table writing in his notebook in the light of an oil lamp. Several large peeled potatoes on the table. He looks up to think but gets interrupted by the sound of a tractor. Stands and heads for the door.*

The camera pulls back as the tractor rumbles in. The rain has stopped, but it's still blowing up rotten from the lake.

PARKIN *dumps logs and* MARWOOD *walks round to his cab. He smiles up at the farmer offering thanks and how much do I owe?*

ISACS PARKIN: You can pay us when you come down.

MARWOOD: What about the chicken?

ISACS PARKIN: He's on the back. In the sack.

55. INT. LIVING ROOM. COTTAGE. EVENING.

MARWOOD *shakes* WITHNAIL *into consciousness. Directs his attention towards a sack on the floor.*

MARWOOD: Parkin's been. There's the supper.

The bag starts to move. Without getting into the mechanics a chicken finds a way out.

WITHNAIL: What are we supposed to do with that?

MARWOOD: Eat it.

WITHNAIL: Eat it. The fucker's alive.

MARWOOD: I know that. You've gotta kill it.

WITHNAIL: Me? I'm the fire lighter and fuel collector.

MARWOOD: I know that. But I got the logs in.

The chicken starts to walk.

WITHNAIL: Follow it.

MARWOOD: It takes away your appetite looking at it.

WITHNAIL: No it doesn't, I'm starving. How can we make it die?

MARWOOD: You have to throttle them.

Suddenly it leaps in the air and momentarily drives them off.
I think you should strangle it instantly, in case it starts
trying to make friends with us.

WITHNAIL: All right, get hold of it. You hold it down, and I'll
strangle it.

MARWOOD: I couldn't. It's got dreadful beady eyes. It's
staring me out.

WITHNAIL: It's a *fucking chicken.* Just think of it with bacon
across its back.

*WITHNAIL's volume propels the chicken into the kitchen. He
follows it, pausing at the kitchen door.*

All right, I'll deal with this, but you'll have to get its guts
out.

56. INT. KITCHEN. COTTAGE. NIGHT.

Firelight in the living room and candlelight in here. MARWOOD
*has finished preparations. A muzzle of a shotgun prods at the back
of his head. He turns and knocks the double barrel aside.*

MARWOOD: Never point guns at people. It's extremely
dangerous. Where'd you get it?

WITHNAIL: Cupboard.

MARWOOD: Well put it back. What about this roasting dish?

WITHNAIL *shakes his head and turns on the chicken with his
gun. The barrels poke at it. It's still in possession of its feet and
a considerable amount of feathers.*

MARWOOD: What are we gonna cook it in?

WITHNAIL: You're the food and plumbings man. I've no idea.
I wish I'd found this an hour ago. I'd have taken great
pleasure in gunning this pullet down.

The gun is lowered and WITHNAIL *applies himself to the
chicken.*

WITHNAIL: Shouldn't it be more bald than that?

MARWOOD: No, it shouldn't. All right, we're gonna have to
reverse the roles. We'll bake the potatoes in the oven, and
boil this bastard over the fire.

*A large iron kettle. They attempt to stuff it in. Head first.
Won't go.* MARWOOD *reverses it. Arse next. Won't go.*

WITHNAIL *punches it. But this pullet is not going to go in this kettle.*

WITHNAIL: Let's get its feet off.

MARWOOD *shakes his head and walks purposefully towards the oven.*

MARWOOD: No, it's gonna need its feet.

He opens the oven door. Instructs WITHNAIL *to remove his boots. They come out steaming on the end of a poker.*

MARWOOD *replaces them with a brick. Positioned side on at the bottom of the oven.*

It can stand with its legs either side of that.

MARWOOD *mounts it upright looking out towards the door.*

WITHNAIL *bastes his hands as another door is slammed in the chicken's face.*

57. EXT. COUNTRYSIDE. DAY.

About as much countryside as a Super Panavision lens is capable of handling. The lake and the sky and the mountains look anaemic. This is a huge panorama. Somewhere in the middle of it is a tiny telephone booth.

WITHNAIL (*V.O.*): I've already put two shillings in. No. I haven't got another. It's not my fault if the system doesn't work.

58. EXT. TELEPHONE BOOTH. COUNTRY ROAD/LAKESIDE. DAY.

WITHNAIL *shoves his head out. Like* MARWOOD *several days' beard.*

WITHNAIL: The bitch hung up on me.

A search for more change begins. WITHNAIL *has none and* MARWOOD *a single two shilling piece. Reluctantly offers it to* WITHNAIL.

MARWOOD: I'll phone tomorrow. I don't wanna call anyway.

MARWOOD *squeezes into the booth to escape the icy wind. Redialling takes effect and* WITHNAIL *is connected surprisingly quickly.*

Don't wanna hear I haven't got it.

A combination of bad line and emotion causes WITHNAIL *to shout.*

WITHNAIL: Hello? How are you? Very well. A what? Why
wouldn't they see me? . . . This is ridiculous, I haven't
been for a job for three months. Understudy Constantine?
I'm not gonna understudy Constantine. Why can't I play
the part? That's ridiculous. No I'm not in London.
Penrith. *Penrith.* Well what about TV? Listen, I pay you
ten per cent to do that. What? Well lick ten per cent of the
asses for me then. Hello? Hello? Hello? How dare you.
Fuck you.

He bashes the receiver down and follows MARWOOD *out of the box.*

Bastard asked me to understudy Constantine in *The Seagull.*
They start walking up the road. MARWOOD *clutching a grocery bag.*

I'm not gonna understudy anybody. Specially that little
pimp. Anyway, I loathe those Russian plays. Always full
of women staring out of windows, whining about ducks
going to Moscow.

59. EXT. TRACK. MOUNTAINSIDE. DAY.

*Sodden fields. The mountains seem to have an inexhaustible supply
of liquids. The reality of agents has depressed them both. They
proceed carefully to avoid puncturing bags.*

WITHNAIL: What d'you think of Desmond Wolfe?

MARWOOD: In respect of what?

WITHNAIL: I'm thinking of changing my name.

MARWOOD: It's too like Donald Wolfit . . .

Pausing for breath, MARWOOD *stops. Thrusts the groceries across.*

Change-over point . . .

WITHNAIL *looks up at the tractor descending from the top fields.*

WITHNAIL: D'you think he's happier than us?

MARWOOD: No.

He opens the gate and WITHNAIL *follows through. They*

52

continue walking. Absorbed in their own thoughts. The tractor is about a hundred yards away. It stops suddenly and ISACS PARKIN *sticks his head out. For some reason he waves frantically and they wave back.*

WITHNAIL: I suppose happiness is relative . . .

ISACS PARKIN *is back in his tractor. Gunning the engine and racing towards them in a haze of mud. And still waving frantically.*

. . . but I never thought it would be a polythene bag without a hole in it.

MARWOOD *isn't listening. Watches* ISACS PARKIN *drive like a maniac.*

MARWOOD: What's the matter with him?

MARWOOD *suddenly swings round. Wide eyed. The question is answered.*

MARWOOD: You didn't shut the gate.

The farmer is driving dangerously. Head stuck out and screaming.

ISACS PARKIN: Shut that gate. Shut that gate.

But it's too late. They stand paralysed in their bags. Watch as the bull charges up the field and crashes through the opening. Stop that bull. Stop that bull.

Thrusting the groceries across WITHNAIL *runs for it and literally dives over the nearest wall.* ISACS PARKIN *leaps from his tractor and poles across the field like Long John Silver.* 'Stop that bull. Stop that bull.' *Five yards separation and the bull stops.* MARWOOD *freezes.* WITHNAIL'*s head comes back over the wall.*

WITHNAIL: Grab its ring.

MARWOOD *holds the groceries out in front of him as though offering some sort of sacrifice. A flimsy barrier between himself and four thousand pounds of angry hamburger waiting to take revenge.*

Keep your bag up. Out vibe it.

With a terrified sneer MARWOOD *stares into its bloodshot eyes. Breath like a Ferrari revving up. Exhaust from either nostril.*

It wants to get up there and fuck those cows.

ISACS PARKIN *arrives but can't get over the wall because of his stiffened leg.* MARWOOD *is the pig in the middle.*

WITHNAIL *looking over the wall the farmer looking over the wall opposite.*

ISACS PARKIN: Show no fear.

The bull starts hoof actions in the mud. MARWOOD *stares in terror. This is quite possibly an advertisement preceding the charge.*

Show no fear. Just run at it.

MARWOOD: That can't be sensible, can it? The bastard's about to run at me.

ISACS PARKIN: He's randy.

MARWOOD: Yes, yes, I know he is.

WITHNAIL: He wants to have sex with those cows.

MARWOOD: Shut up Withnail.

ISACS PARKIN: Run at it shouting.

WITHNAIL: Do as he says. Start shouting.

Seems like the shouting is imminent anyway. Also the running. The only concern troubling MARWOOD *is the direction the running is advised. On the edge of vision he sees* WITHNAIL *light a cigarette!*

WITHNAIL: It won't gore you.

MARWOOD's *voice sounds like Richard III at some sort of climax.*

MARWOOD: A coward, you are, Withnail. An expert on bulls, you are not.

This statement is delivered with considerable emotion.

Violence towards WITHNAIL *drives* MARWOOD *towards the bull. Vegetables fly as he descends in his carrier bags shouting at the top of his voice. The bull is astonished by what's coming at him. Apparently even less prepared to get charged than charge himself. He turns instantly and hot hoofs it back through the opening.* PARKIN *hobbles at speed and closes the gate behind him. As soon as he's convinced the danger is over* WITHNAIL *clambers back over the wall.*

MARWOOD *is trembling and in a state of shock. He picks*

up stray vegetables from the mud. PARKIN *shouts* 'Keep this gate shut.' *And legs off as though he has just finished the shit/crop allocation in time for tea.*

WITHNAIL: I think an evening at the Crow.

MARWOOD *grabs a turnip. The experience has frozen his senses.*

MARWOOD: An evening at the Crow? I could have been killed.

WITHNAIL: Nahh. Parkin knew what he was doing.

MARWOOD: Sure he did. An absolute fucking authority. That's why he couldn't get over the wall.

WITHNAIL: Don't wanna overdo it, do you?

Both daylight and the image are dissolving as they head up the hill.

WITHNAIL: We're in the countryside. Things like this are perfectly normal.

60. INT. LIVING ROOM. COTTAGE. EVENING.

The dissolve completes into candlelight and firelight. MARWOOD *sits in front of the latter writing in his notebook with the assistance of the former. Big shadows on the wall behind him.* WITHNAIL *is fencing with himself again. Got a cigarette stuck in his maw. Decides to involve* MARWOOD *in the exercise and starts prodding selected areas of his back and neck.* MARWOOD *swats him off like an unwelcome wasp. But the wasp comes back.*

WITHNAIL: C'mon . . . on your pins.

MARWOOD: Stop it. I'm thinking.

The point of the épée pokes the very centre of MARWOOD'S *head.*

WITHNAIL: C'mon. 'Here's my fiddlestick; here's that shall make you dance!'

And he prods and pokes further selected areas of MARWOOD'S *body. With increasing annoyance the recipient knocks the épée away.* WITHNAIL *removes his cigarette to intone à la Shakespeare.*

WITHNAIL: Oh calm, dishonourable, vile submission! Come on, you rat-catcher, will you walk?

MARWOOD: Last time I fought you, I thrashed you into the
  ground.
WITHNAIL: Thou speakest bollocks. C'mon.
  MARWOOD *is suddenly on his feet, retrieves another épée from*
  the walking-stick tub. Now he's facing WITHNAIL *across the*
  table.
MARWOOD: All right, Withnail. Prepare to die. Three hits to
  win, loser buys the drinks.
  Here comes some Errol Flynn – and if it's spelt wrong
  it's because it's fought wrong. But these boys can
  fence – evidently part of their drama school training. I'm not
  going to describe it because I don't know what it'll look like till
  we're there. But MARWOOD *gets a poke, 'One' into*
  WITHNAIL'*s throttle, which enrages him. Fag still burning*
  he lunges at the coat hooks and grabs the mask. 'Right, you
  bastard', *and the mask goes on.*
    The fight continues. WITHNAIL *has donned the mask with*
  his cigarette still in his mouth – a thing like a smoking beehive
  is slashing around the premises. MARWOOD *finally wins.*
  WITHNAIL *takes* 'Three' *and is down on the table point in*
  his neck – 'Yield? Yield?' *And he does yield.*

61. EXT. COUNTRY ROAD. NIGHT.
WITHNAIL *and* MARWOOD *pound along in the moonlight. A*
spiteful wind coming off the lake. Also reflections of a tiny village.
Their destination is one of the few buildings emitting light.
MARWOOD (*V.O.*): If the Crow and Cunt ever had life it was
  dead now. It was like walking into a lung. A
  sulphur-stained nicotine-yellow and fly-blown lung. Its
  landlord was a retired alcoholic with military pretensions
  and a complexion like the inside of a tea pot.

62. INT. CROW AND CUNT. PUBLIC HOUSE. NIGHT.
A pair of small rooms with a log fire at one end and a bar in the
middle. Thick smoke and packed with men, mainly wankers from
the local farms. One or two shepherds. Everything is yellow except
for the landlord who is bright red. Years of consistent boozing have

gone into this face. It also has a large moustache. WITHNAIL *and* MARWOOD *squat on stools at the bar in front of him.*

MARWOOD (*V.O.*): By the time the doors opened he was arse-holed on rum, and got progressively more arse-holed till he could take no more and fell over about twelve o'clock.

WITHNAIL: We'll have another pair of large Scotches.

They watch in fascination as the GENERAL *lunges for his bottles. He hands them the drinks and turns to his till to ring up. The money drawer shoots out. Catches him in the gut and he staggers. Ricocheting off the bar he throws himself on the till. Grabs a fistful of change and slaps it on the counter.*

THE GENERAL: I thought I was going for a minute . . .

His voice is circa 1942 with faint undertones of Mancunian. But no man has ever put me down. Have you had training in the martial arts?

WITHNAIL: Yes, as a matter of fact I have. Before I became a journalist, I was in the Territorials.

The GENERAL *attempts to focus on* WITHNAIL *with his sepia eyes.*

THE GENERAL: D'you know, when you first came in here, I knew you'd been a services man. You can never disguise it.

A cigarette is offered and WITHNAIL *lights up like Jack the Lad.*

WITHNAIL: What were you in?

THE GENERAL: Tanks. North Africa Corps. A little before your time. Don't spose you've engaged, have you?

WITHNAIL: Ireland . . .

THE GENERAL: Ah, a crack at the Mick.

WITHNAIL: Exactly. We'll have a couple more.

THE GENERAL: These shall be my pleasure.

He swings their glasses under the bottle and repositions them. What are you doing up here, then?

WITHNAIL: Feature for *Country Life*. We're doing a survey of rural types. You know, farmers, travelling tinkers, milkmen, that sort of thing.

Steadying himself on the bar the GENERAL *leans in on* WITHNAIL *as though trying to get the end of his moustache into his ear.*

THE GENERAL: Have you met Jake?

WITHNAIL shakes his head and backs away from a disturbing exhalation from the landlord's gut. His tone is almost conspiratorial.

Poacher. Works the lake. But keep it under your hat.

With what is virtually a salute WITHNAIL *acknowledges this confidence and they make their way to corner seats near the fire.*

The image is soft focus and sideways. It is from the GENERAL's *point of view. As he straightens up it straightens up. Focus improves and he looks across his now nearly empty establishment, calling* 'Time, Gentlemen.'

All the shepherds and wankers have gone home. The fire has gone out. Only WITHNAIL *and* MARWOOD *in front of its embers.* MARWOOD *looks across. The* GENERAL *is supporting himself on the beer pumps like a man on crutches. His jaw is firmly clenched.*

MARWOOD: I think he means it.

The time has approached when they're all too pissed to know what time it is. WITHNAIL *finishes his drink and they stand to leave.*

The door swings open and an alarming-looking creature walks in. Around his neck are a dozen mole traps linked to a length of sisal rope that disappears into his hunchback. Loops of string are tied under his knees. Above them a pair of massive bulges like deformed thigh muscles. This is obviously JAKE *the poacher.*

They watch as he heads for the bar. Pulls his own pint and downs it as quickly as a pint can be poured from a glass. A formidable sight. Like a tree has uprooted itself and come in because it fancied a drink. But respect from the GENERAL. *He gets himself upright to pull the next pint. These drinks are evidently free. A detail that doesn't go unnoticed.* WITHNAIL *leads the way across.*

A pair of Scotches are ordered. And delivered. And on the house. JAKE's *clothes are a mixture of earth and tweed and blood and decaying vegetables. A stink comes off them buckling* MARWOOD's *nostrils.* JAKE *is half-way through his pint when his bulges move. It causes him discomfort. Plunging a hand under his belt he extracts a pair of half-dead eels. They take a terrible bashing on the counter and return to the interior of his trouser. A pair of astonished faces stare.* MARWOOD *leans into* WITHNAIL *with a whisper.*

MARWOOD: Ask him if we can have one.

WITHNAIL: What for?

MARWOOD: So we can eat it. We're fed up with stew.

WITHNAIL *moves in and addresses* JAKE *as though he were a waiter.*

WITHNAIL: Excuse me. Could we have an eel?

The tree turns towards him. Doesn't like the look of this prat. You've got eels down your leg.

JAKE: You leave them alone. Ain't nothin' down there interest to you.

Ignoring WITHNAIL *he returns to his elbows and beer. Finishes his pint and suddenly tugs at the rope vanishing into his hump.*

Help I, Raymond Goff. These be fed from ass-'ole to beak.

The GENERAL *grabs at the rope. With difficulty he pulls a brace of pheasant over* JAKE's *head and conceals them behind the bar. More astonishment from* MARWOOD *and* WITHNAIL. *And more whispers.*

The poacher gestures towards the whisky. Everyone gets a glass.

MARWOOD: What about one of those pheasants?

WITHNAIL *is reluctant.* JAKE *is preparing to leave. Now or never.*

Go on. Ask him.

The GENERAL *collapses on a stack of beer crates.* JAKE *rattles his traps and ties his coat with the rope.* WITHNAIL *works a smile.*

WITHNAIL: Excuse me. We were wondering whether we could purchase a pheasant off of you?

JAKE: No . . . I ain't got nothin' to sell.

WITHNAIL: Come on, old boy. What's in your hump?

JAKE *puts his face into* WITHNAIL. *Skin like the sole of a foot.*

JAKE: Now look you here. Them pheasants there are fer his pot. These eels is fer my pot. What makes you think I should give ya summat fer yer pot?

WITHNAIL: What pot?

MARWOOD: Our cooking pot.

JAKE: Arr, he knows. Give I wheeze on that fag.

MARWOOD *hands the cigarette across.* JAKE *sucks a deep inhalation. He hands it back and* MARWOOD *ashtrays it for fear of contamination. A Gauloise is offered.* JAKE *takes three. Wraps them in his hanky.*

I might see you lads in the week. I might put a rabbit your way.

WITHNAIL: We don't want a rabbit. We want a pheasant.

JAKE: Now look you here ya young prat, I ain't got no pheasants. I ain't got no birds, no more an' you do.

WITHNAIL: Of course you have. You're the poacher.

Not a very sensitive remark. JAKE *is clearly upset by this accusation. Exploring his trousers he withdraws one of his eels.*

JAKE: If I hear more wordsa you. I'll put one a these here black pods on yer.

The eel wraps itself up Jake's arm. A rapid retreat as he menaces the creature in WITHNAIL's *face.*

WITHNAIL: Don't threaten me with a dead fish.

JAKE: Half-dead he might be. But I'll come on up after ye, and wake you up with a live one.

WITHNAIL: Sod your pheasants. You'll have to find us first.

WITHNAIL's *indignation has propelled him to the door. As* MARWOOD *follows him through* JAKE *raises his voice to bid them farewell.*

JAKE: Oh, I know where you are. You two's up at Crow Crag. I been watchin' you. Especially you, prancin' like a tit.

63. EXT. MOUNTAIN TRACK. OVER LAKE. NIGHT.
Several superior brains have dealt with nights like this. Here are raging moons and starry-starry nights. MARWOOD *and* WITHNAIL *labour through the mire. The latter breathless and staggering.*

WITHNAIL: If I see that silage heap hanging around up here, I'll take the bastard axe to him.
The cottage comes into sight. Indigo slates in the moonlight.
WITHNAIL *staggers to a wall and shouts at five miles of lake.*
Bastards. Bastards. Bastards.
Nobody to reply except an echo. As loud and as drunk as he is.
You'll all suffer. (Suffer. Suffer. Suffer.) I'll show the lot of you. (You. You. You.) I'm gonna be a star. (Star. Star. Star. Star. Star.)
He turns away and the echo fades into the black and starry night.

64. INT. LIVING ROOM. COTTAGE. DAY.
A load of weather on the roof. A large fire in the grate. MARWOOD *is stirring in the kettle. Fishes something out. Tastes it and decides it's ready.* WITHNAIL *is at the dining table. Already hacked one crust off and is working at the opposite end of the loaf. A complaint from* MARWOOD *as he transfers kettle to table.*

MARWOOD: What are you doing?
WITHNAIL: Getting the crusts. I like the crusts.
MARWOOD: So do I. You can have that one. The other one's mine when we get to it.
MARWOOD *sits and* WITHNAIL *peers into the kettle.*
WITHNAIL: Vegetables again? We'll sprout fucking feelers soon. Must be twenty thousand sheep out there on those fucking volcanoes, and we got a plateful of carrots.
MARWOOD: There's black puddings in it.
WITHNAIL: Black puddings are no good to us.
He suddenly pushes his plate aside and rises to his feet.
I want something's flesh!

61

65. EXT. MOUNTAINSIDE. MOUNTAIN STREAM. DAY.
The water is freezing and fast running and so is WITHNAIL.
*With bare feet and trousers rolled up above his knees he charges
up the centre of the stream loosing off his shotgun. Massive
explosions of water. A single fish is atomised.* MARWOOD *stands
in his bags on the bank watching. Sees another fish. Directs*
WITHNAIL *who fires. Empty gun. He reloads. Fires. The fish
has gone.*

66. EXT. HILLSIDE TRACK. DAY.
*Late afternoon. They walk fishless through the fields. Both are
bagless. Both dejected. Even the sheep look pissed off.*
WITHNAIL: I think I'll call myself Donald Twain.
> *They turn off the track and head down the hillside towards the
> cottage. About twenty yards above it when* WITHNAIL
> *commands 'Stop.' With knees bent he goes into a sort of
> running crouch to a wall.*
>
> MARWOOD *follows. 'Keep down. He'll see you.' They
> both peer over the wall. A dark bundle of overcoat and savage
> hair is squinting into the living room window of the cottage.
> Hard to identify at first. Then no mistaking it. To*
> WITHNAIL's *horror it is* JAKE, *armed with a shotgun.*
WITHNAIL: It's him. What does he want?
MARWOOD: Better get down there and ask him.
> *He attempts to stand.* WITHNAIL *pulls him down. Fear in
> the larynx.*
WITHNAIL: Don't be a fool! He's got a gun. The bastard's
psychotic, you've only gotta look at him.
> JAKE *is evidently tired of his investigations and is heading
> back towards the lake. He stops and turns for a last look and
> they cautiously climb the wall with* WITHNAIL *muttering
> about precautions.*

67. INT. LIVING ROOM. (KITCHEN). COTTAGE. NIGHT.
MARWOOD *is in front of the fire reading a play* Journey's End *by
R. C. Sherriff.* WITHNAIL *has produced a huge rusty bolt from
somewhere and nails it to the kitchen door. Security is completed*

with a shovel rammed under the door knob. He then loads the
shotgun and returns to the living room.

WITHNAIL: This place has become impossible.

A sinister wind slams night doors. MARWOOD *ignores the
diatribe.*

Freezing cold . . . perpetual rain . . . and now a fucking
madman on the prowl outside, with eels.

MARWOOD: All right, you've made your point. We'll pack up
and get out tomorrow.

Their boots stand in the grate and socks stand next to them.

MARWOOD *tests one of his. Baked stiff. Starts putting it on.*

WITHNAIL: What are you doing?

MARWOOD: Going for a slash.

WITHNAIL: No you're not. You can't. I can't get my boots on
when they're hot.

MARWOOD: I'll go alone.

WITHNAIL *doesn't like the sound of this and rockets to his
feet.*

WITHNAIL: No you won't. You're not leaving me in here
alone. Those are the kind of windows faces look in at.

68. INT. STAIRWAY. COTTAGE. NIGHT.

Owls and wind and doors banging. Candlelight on the stairs.

WITHNAIL: In both our interests I think we should sleep
together.

MARWOOD: Don't be ridiculous. He's not coming up here in
the dark.

MARWOOD *opens a window at the top of the stairs and takes
a piss.*

WITHNAIL: Of course he is. He's on that lake every night.
And if he decides to come up here and catches one of us
unawares, he's got a much better chance of dealing with
the other.

MARWOOD: No.

He closes the window followed by his bedroom door on
WITHNAIL.

69. INT. BEDROOM. COTTAGE. NIGHT.

MARWOOD *is obviously in the middle of a pleasant dream.*
Occasionally chuckling in his sleep. The door opens and a candle
comes in followed by WITHNAIL *and shotgun.* MARWOOD *starts*
back as he wakes. Blinks at this spectrelike figure in Y-fronts.

WITHNAIL: What's the matter with you?

> MARWOOD *is too drowsy to answer.* WITHNAIL *is drenched*
> *in terror.*

What are you laughing at?

MARWOOD: I was dreaming. What d'you want?

WITHNAIL: You frightened the piss out of me. Move over.
I'm getting in.

> MARWOOD *resists but a pocked leg forces itself under the*
> *covers. A brief struggle follows.* WITHNAIL *manages to get*
> *into the bed.*
>
> > *Huge shadows in the candlelight. A dispute over the*
> > *blankets. It resolves itself with* MARWOOD's *arse thrust in the*
> > *icy air.*

MARWOOD: This is ridiculous. I'll have to sleep in your bed.

WITHNAIL: I'll have to come with you then.

MARWOOD: Will you get out?

WITHNAIL: No.

MARWOOD: Then I will.

> *They both get out together. Stare at each other. Both get back*
> *in together.* MARWOOD *is prepared to tolerate* WITHNAIL
> *but not his shotgun. It's positioned across the bed below their*
> *chins.*

All right. You can stay. But the gun doesn't.

WITHNAIL: I must keep the gun. I intend to remain awake till
morning.

> MARWOOD *snaps up in the bed. Attempts to confiscate the*
> *shotgun.*

MARWOOD: This is my bed, and I demand precedence in it.
Give me the gun.

WITHNAIL: No.

> *A fight in the bed begins. Little to see but two heads and a*
> *muzzle and a heap of writhing blankets. The gun goes off.*

Blows a fucking great hole in the wall behind the bed. A paralysis. Silence. Smoke and dust settle. Then MARWOOD *emerges with an explosion as violent as the gun. 'You mad fucking bastard.' He storms across the room and launches the weapon head first through the window. A shattering of glass. Then this terrific door slam as he pounds out to sleep in* WITHNAIL's *room.*

70. INT. BEDROOM. COTTAGE. NIGHT.
A door banging as wind blunders to the lake. Owls hooting in the distance. MARWOOD *is asleep. The door opens. The candle comes in followed by* WITHNAIL. *Face ruptured with terror. The candle goes down on the bedside table and a hand clamps over* MARWOOD's *mouth.* MARWOOD *wakes choking for breath and the hand gets bashed aside.* WITHNAIL *dances around. Finger over lips. A gesture for silence.*

MARWOOD: Get out. Fuck you. Fuck off.
With hands waving like a hypnotist WITHNAIL *screams in a whisper.*
WITHNAIL: Shut up. Listen. Listen.
MARWOOD tries to focus his ears and eyes but manages only temper.
MARWOOD: There's nothing. Get to bed.
He hunches back under the blankets. WITHNAIL *decides to join him.*
WITHNAIL: I heard a noise. I must get in.
MARWOOD: Oh, for fuck's sake.
WITHNAIL gets into the bed. MARWOOD *turns over. There is a noise.*
What was that?
WITHNAIL: That's it. That's it.
MARWOOD: What is it?
WITHNAIL: It's the maniac.
MARWOOD sits up. Myopic ears straining at the darkness. The door continues to bang. But nothing suspicious and the noise has gone.
MARWOOD: Probably foxes looking for grub.

WITHNAIL *suddenly stiffens in the bed. Knocks the candle over which extinguishes as it hits the floor. Faint moonlight now illuminates the room.*

WITHNAIL: Listen. Listen.

No mistaking it this time. Definitely a suspicious movement outside. Here come the wide eyes and sweat. Both are now bolt upright in the bed. Hearts revving up as the adrenalin squirts in. Sound re-invades the silence. Unmistakably the grind of gravel under the heel of a heavy boot. An exchange of tiny whispers.

MARWOOD: Maybe it's the farmer.

WITHNAIL: At two o'clock in the morning? It's the killer. He's come to kill us. What are we gonna do?

The feet are heading round the house towards the kitchen door. A rattle and a banging as the intruder shakes the securities. He wants to come in. He's trying to get in.

MARWOOD: Be quiet. He can't. He'll go away.

They follow the footsteps with their ears. After several indecisive tramplings they get fainter and move away from the house.

MARWOOD: He's going . . .

WITHNAIL *has gone up six octaves. Like a whispering choir boy.*

WITHNAIL: This is all your fault. You've even given him the fucking gun.

For a few moments a silence that promises perpetuality. Then both are shattered with the glass of the living room window. He's coming through the fucking window. He's getting in.

An aggressive grunt downstairs as the intruder attempts to force his way in. WITHNAIL *is stiff as a board and practically levitating. Though* MARWOOD *is equally terrified, he plans some sort of defence. Grabs the candle.* 'Gimme the matches.' *A Walt Disney mouse replies.* 'Downstairs.' *And so is Jake. They hear his feet make contact with the stone floor. Then again profound silence.* WITHNAIL *vices a hand on to* MARWOOD. *Gurgles* 'He's in.' *And then shoves the sheet in*

Uncle Monty pays a surprise visit.

his mouth. They stare into the boulders of silence. Then a
hair-raising panic-striking sound. WITHNAIL *gags through*
the sheet. 'He's sharpening a fucking knife.'

MARWOOD: We'll have to tackle him. You stay in bed and
pretend to be asleep. He'll go for you. When he does I'll
leap on his back.

MARWOOD *attempts to implement his plan but* WITHNAIL
detains him.

WITHNAIL: No. No. It'll be too late. I'll be knifed by then.
We'll have to try and make friends with him.

The latch clicks on the door at the bottom of the stairs. Then a
creak of wood as footsteps mount. Slow heavy treads of
unfamiliarity with the house. A pause. They head for
MARWOOD's *room.*

  Although WITHNAIL *is atrophied with fear he pushes at*
MARWOOD's *back with marshmallow arms. Interprets Jake's*
direction as a signal of his intentions.

WITHNAIL: He's gone into your room. It's you he wants.
Offer him yourself.

A terrible moment of silence. Then the feet head back. The bed
is thrashing the wall in record of their heart beats. The door
knob turns. A yellow beam of torch light. A low sustained
rattle escapes WITHNAIL's *throat. Like a death rattle. The*
cry of a coward in crisis. Perhaps he's just died of a heart
attack.

  Heads press back into the pillows. The beam dazzles their
eyes. A voice tangled with saliva and grinding teeth attempts
speech. Several breathless grunts before he falls back in the
pillow.

WITHNAIL: We mean no harm . . .

The beam lowers itself. A chuckle. A towering figure. It
speaks.

MONTY: Dear boys. Dear boys. Forgive me.

Total silence. Followed by total relief. Followed by total
anger.

MARWOOD: Monty. Monty. Monty.

WITHNAIL: Monty. You terrible cunt!

MONTY: Forgive me. It was inconsiderate of me not to have
    telegrammed.
WITHNAIL: What are you doing? Prowling around in the
    middle of the fucking night?
    *WITHNAIL's bark redirects his uncle's torch. He coyly
    examines the floorboards. Clearly he thinks he's disturbed
    them at it.*
MONTY: I had a punctured tyre. I had to wait an aeon for
    assistance. I'm sorry if I disturbed you. I should have
    knocked. I'll sleep in the spare room tonight if I
    may.
MARWOOD: Anywhere you like.

71. INT. LIVING ROOM. COTTAGE. DAY.
*Sounds of chopping outside. Squares of sunshine on the wall. An
unusual sight. The first clear day. Apart from socks and boots
MARWOOD walks in fully dressed. An almost remarkable
transformation. He scans the changes as he applies his boots. Floor
swept and fire blazing. A huge bowl of fruit on the table. No
broken windows. Monty has worked magic in here. Elbowing his
coat MARWOOD walks into the kitchen.*

*Work surfaces scrubbed. Floor mopped. A stack of exclusive
groceries on the table. And under it a cardboard box containing
several joints of meat. Monty clearly intends to stay for a while.
And here he is. Plus fours. Hiking boots. And an armful of logs.*
MONTY: Good morning. Did you sleep well?
    *MARWOOD follows him into the living room. MONTY dumps
    the wood.*
    I do apologise for last night. It was perfectly inconsiderate
    of me.
MARWOOD: Perfectly all right, Monty. You've been busy in
    here?
MONTY: As a bee.
    *He cavorts back into the kitchen. And unwraps a deck of
    bacon.*
MARWOOD: How did you repair the window?
MONTY: I didn't break it. Merely forced it a little. Sorry if I

frightened you, there was an empty wine bottle on the
ledge.
MONTY *prods rashers with a fork. An exercise he doesn't
enjoy.*
Why don't you go and wake him? Breakfast in fifteen
minutes.

72. INT. LIVING ROOM. COTTAGE. DAY.
The improvements in living standards haven't gone unnoticed by
WITHNAIL. *Breakfast has matured into Turkish cigarettes.*
MONTY *beams with pleasure.*

   *An appropriate moment for a rendition of Alfred, Lord
Tennyson.*

MONTY: The old order changeth, yielding place to new. And
   God fulfils himself in many ways. And soon, I suppose, I
   shall be swept away by some vulgar little tumor.
   *The moment mists his eyes. His head shakes. His voice
   vaporises.*
   Ah, my boys, my boys, we're at the end of an age. We live
   in a land of weather forecasts, and breakfasts that 'set in'.
   Shat on by Tories. Shovelled up by Labour. And here we
   are. We three. Perhaps the last island of beauty in the
   world.
   *He takes their hands. For a moment it seems he's going to
   shove them in his mouth. An exchange of eyes. And then*
   MONTY *smiles.*
   Now which one of you is going to be a splendid fellow and
   go down to the Rolls for the rest of the things?
   MARWOOD *and* WITHNAIL *stand simultaneously and speak
   simultaneously.*
MARWOOD/WITHNAIL: I will.
MARWOOD: No, I'd better go. I've got to see about digging the
   car out, anyway.
MONTY: We have my car, dear boy.
MARWOOD: Yes, but if it rains, we're buggered.
   Or words to that effect. MONTY *doesn't notice.* MARWOOD
   stutters.

70

MARWOOD: I mean . . . we'll never get it out . . .

MONTY: Stranded!

A surprising enthusiasm from WITHNAIL *as he reaches for his bags.*

WITHNAIL: We'll deal with the car when I get back. Leave this to me.

MARWOOD: I'll come with you then. I fancy a walk.

MONTY: No, No. I'm told you're a little wizard in the kitchen. I'll need you to work on the joint.

WITHNAIL: Yeah. You're the cook.

MONTY raises an eyebrow as WITHNAIL *begins shaking out his footwear.*

We forgot to bring Wellingtons . . .

MONTY: But how dreadful. You mean you've been up here in all this beastly mud and oomska without Wellingtons? WITHNAIL *nods and heads for the kitchen door.* MONTY *follows. And somewhat peeved* MARWOOD *paces after them.* WITHNAIL *tramps outside and* MARWOOD *sees them both through the kitchen window.*

This afternoon I'm going to take you both into Penrith, and get you fitted with some good-quality rubber boots.

73. INT. KITCHEN. COTTAGE. DAY.

MARWOOD *seems worried to be alone with the uncle. They're both midway through unpacking the supplies. A bombardment of smiles from* MONTY *every time their eyes meet.* MARWOOD *does his best to return them. But nerves force lips into a sort of sneer.* MONTY *uses a napkin to remove a massive leg of lamb from his box. He shoves it at* MARWOOD *who holds it like a father with his newly born baby.* MONTY *chirps towards another box.*

MONTY: Garlic, rosemary and salt.

He plunges into a grocery sack. A tablecloth and napkins and a pair of aprons. Slips into one. Goes for MARWOOD *with the other.*

MONTY: I brought two in case either of you was any good in the kitchen.

MARWOOD: I'm not.

MONTY: Of course you are. Cooking's one of the natural instincts.

He heads for him with the apron. MARWOOD *defends with his leg.*

MARWOOD: Listen Monty, this is all very kind of you, but I really think I ought to get out there and get some work done on the car . . .

MONTY: Nonsense, you haven't time. We'll be having a late luncheon at three.

MARWOOD *would say anything to avoid the apron. Says the first thing that comes into his head. It is said with great regret.*

MARWOOD: 'Fraid we have to leave by three, Monty.

MONTY: Leave?

MARWOOD: Yes, didn't he tell you? We've gotta get back to sign on.

MONTY: Sign on? At a Labour Exchange?

But you're successful actors? They realise the blunder together.

MARWOOD: It's sort of fashionable, actually. All the actors do it. Even Redgrave.

MONTY: But surely you could forgo for just this one occasion? I've come a very long way to see you both.

MONTY'S *eyes bulge behind his glasses.* MARWOOD *affects remorse.*

MARWOOD: Well, no. Can't really. I mean, I'd love to stay. But he's more adamant to get back than I am.

MONTY: Then we must choose our moment, and have a word with him. I'm sure together we could persuade him.

MARWOOD *suddenly finds himself entering into some sort of pact.*

Now slip this on.

MONTY *has both the problem and* MARWOOD *in hand. The apron goes on.* MARWOOD *is tied up at the back and* MONTY *returns to his work.*

Garlic, rosemary and salt. I can never touch meat until it's cooked. As a youth I used to weep in butcher's shops.

MARWOOD *transfers his meat to the table and reluctantly begins a search for the condiments. Garlic and salt come out.* 'I can't find the rosemary.' *Feigning exasperation* MONTY *launches beans at the sink and approaches wiping his hands on the apron.* MARWOOD *attempts to get out of his way. Out of luck instead.* MONTY *circles him in his arms and forces him backwards over the table. Their faces come to the point where they normally kiss in films.*

MONTY: I'm sure we can find it together.

MARWOOD continues to arc backwards as MONTY *searches behind him.*

MARWOOD: Perhaps it's in the other bag?

MONTY: Perhaps it is. Shall we look?

Before they do WITHNAIL *barges in. Dumps groceries on the table.*

WITHNAIL: Oh – sorry. Sherry's in there.

He gestures towards a carrier bag and continues into the living room as though he'd disturbed the courting couple. MONTY *doesn't seem at all concerned. Breaks away to deal with the sherry.* MARWOOD *follows* WITHNAIL. *A fast and frenetic exchange of whispers.*

MARWOOD: What d'you mean 'sorry'? What's going on? What's he doing here?

WITHNAIL collapses into an armchair and begins removing his bags.

We can't stay. He won't leave me alone.

Further exchange is cut off by MONTY. *He lumbers in with three glasses of differing style and an opened bottle of Bristol Cream.*

MONTY: I'm afraid we must drink from these.

The glasses are handed out and MONTY *moves over them with sherry.*

I trust their shape will not offend your palate . . .

MONTY slips the wink at MARWOOD *and proposes an expansive toast.*

To a delightful weekend in the country.

The glasses go up. A clink. A drink. Everyone is happy but MARWOOD.

74. INT. JAG/MOUNTAINSIDE. TRACK. DAY.
Effortless sunlight. An amateur photographer's day. MARWOOD
and WITHNAIL *are in the process of salvaging the Jag.*
MARWOOD: You were the one who wanted to leave.
WITHNAIL: You were the one who wanted to stay.
MARWOOD: Well, we can't. You saw him. He practically
    kissed me.
WITHNAIL: All right, we'll get the lunch down, and
    afterwards I'll have a word with him and we'll leave.
    MONTY *appears from the house with a teasing remonstration.*
MONTY: You foolish boys. What on earth possessed you to
    bring a car up here?
    He starts waving his arms about. Points to a parking spot.
    Get it over there, and we'll travel in the Rolls.

75. EXT. COUNTRY ROAD. DAY.
*With Charlie Kunz supplying the music the Roller winds down a
hill. Boys in the back and Monty driving. A small country town
appears in the distance.*
MONTY (*V.O.*): I do think you could have shaved. What on
    earth will people think of me turning up with you two.
    You look like a pair of farm-hands.

76. EXT. MARKET SQUARE. PENRITH. DAY.
Surprise from the locals as everyone gets out. WITHNAIL *and*
MARWOOD *with their dishevelled appearance.* MONTY *with his
watch and waistcoat and radish in his lapel. Residents actually
stop and stare.*
MONTY: This is most embarrassing. Let's get away from the
    car.
    Beetling off he crosses the square with them following.
    MONTY *brakes and a wallet comes out. A pair of crisp blue
    notes are dispersed. He shoves a glance towards the Penrith
    Tea Rooms.*
MONTY: Buy the Wellingtons and I'm going to buy some
    razors and shaving soap, and I'll see you over there in half
    an hour.

And off he fucks. MARWOOD *examines the loot as*
WITHNAIL *arrives.*

MARWOOD: Pair of blues. One each.

WITHNAIL *flexes his fiver and is infused with a sudden
inspiration.*

WITHNAIL: I think a drink, don't you?

MARWOOD: What about the Wellingtons?

WITHNAIL: Bollocks to the Wellingtons.

*They cross the cobbles, heading towards King Henry's public
house.*

We'll tell him they had a farmers' conference and had a
run on them.

77. INT. KING HENRY'S PUB. SALOON BAR. DAY.

A dingy little establishment. WITHNAIL *sits alone at the bar in
front of a pair of half-drunk pints. His eyes study a mirror reflecting*
MARWOOD *making a telephone call half-way down a hallway.
The receiver goes down and* MARWOOD *reappears looking
despondent.*

MARWOOD: Hasn't heard a thing. Apparently they're still
seeing people.

WITHNAIL: You don't wanna go to Manchester, anyway. Play
a bloody soldier?

MARWOOD: Don't I? I damned well do. It's a damned good
little theatre.

WITHNAIL: Not much of a part though, is it?

MARWOOD: Better than nothing.

WITHNAIL: They'd make you cut your hair off.

MARWOOD: So what. You'd lose a leg.

WITHNAIL *finishes his pint. The* BARMAN *informs them*
'Time Gents.'

WITHNAIL: All right, we're gonna have to work quickly. A
pair of quadruple whiskies, and another pair of pints
please.

78. EXT. MARKET SQUARE. PENRITH. DAY.

Speed of consumption has affected speed of inebriation.

WITHNAIL *shuffles up the pavement. A lack of Monty produces indignation.*

WITHNAIL: Where is he? I'm utterly arse-holed.

MARWOOD: We're early.

> *He nods towards the tea rooms on the other side of the square.*
> We wanna get in there, don't we? Eat some cake. Soak up the booze.

79. INT. PENRITH TEA ROOMS. DAY.

A bell on a spring clatters above their heads. All eyes turn in their direction. Not an eyeball in here under seventy years old. Maybe five or six ladies eating dainty little cakes with dainty little forks. The place is dainty. Decorated like one of its iced and jujubed numbers in the window. An OLD WOMAN *in an apron approaches as* WITHNAIL *gestures towards a gingham-clothed table.*

WITHNAIL: All right here?

OLD WOMAN: What do you want?

WITHNAIL: Cake. All right here?

> *Clearly a pair of drunken dustmen. She shows considerable courage.*

OLD WOMAN: No. We're closing in a minute.

WITHNAIL: We're leaving in a minute.

> *They sit down and* WITHNAIL *studies the menu. An old man with a neck lagged in bandage like the top of a boiler glares at them.* WITHNAIL *ignores him and pokes a finger at the 'Afternoon Teas'.*
> We'll have cake and tea.
> *The* BOILER *gets up, balancing on his walking stick.*

BOILER: Didn't you hear? She said she's closed.

> *Insubordination, and the* BOILER *approaches red of face.*
> What do you want in here?

WITHNAIL: Cake. What's it to do with you?

BOILER: I happen to be the proprietor. Now would you leave?

WITHNAIL: Ah, I'm glad you're the proprietor. I was gonna have to have a word with you anyway. We're working on a film up here. Locations see. We might wanna do a film in here.

76

BOILER: You're drunk.

MARWOOD: Just bring out the cakes.

WITHNAIL: Cakes and fine wines.

This is a desperate situation. But the OLD WOMAN *has a solution.*

OLD WOMAN: If you don't leave, we'll call the police.

A threat that brings a flutter of agreement from the feathers in the hats and the pugs on leads faction.

WITHNAIL: Balls. We want the finest wines available to humanity. And we want them *here*. And we want them *now*.

BOILER: Miss Blenehassitt. Telephone the police.

MARWOOD: All right, Miss Blenehassitt, I'm warning you. If you do, you're fired. We'll buy this place and fire you immediately. We're multi-millionaires . . .

MARWOOD *and* WITHNAIL *rise to their feet and the* BOILER *steps back.*

WITHNAIL: Yes, we'll buy this place. And we'll get a fucking juke-box in here to liven all these stiffs up a bit.

BOILER: The police, Miss Blenehassitt.

She goes about it. Fumbles nervously with the phone. Bit of chat from the hats and pugs. 'Vagabonds.' 'They won't like the police.'

Just say there are two drunks in the Penrith Tea Rooms and we want them removed.

MARWOOD: We're not drunks. We're multi-millionaires.

BOILER: Hurry, up, Mabs. We'll keep them here till they arrive.

Seems like he's going to bolt the door. A whispered explanation.

HAT AND PUG: He'll keep them talking.

WITHNAIL: He won't keep us anywhere. We'll buy this place and have it knocked down.

Just as Mabs says 'Police please' *a limousine appears outside.*

MARWOOD: Don't bother. Our car's arrived. We're going.

Eyes alternate between them and the car as they reach the door.

WITHNAIL: But we'll be back. We're coming back in here.

The BOILER *and the* OLD WOMAN *and the old* LADIES *with the feathers and dogs on leads watch in amazement as* WITHNAIL *and* MARWOOD *stagger out and slump in the back of an immaculate Rolls-Royce.*

80. INT. LIVING ROOM. COTTAGE. DAY.
The lamb is sizzling to perfection. WITHNAIL *draws air over his teeth. Closes the oven door.* MARWOOD *appears from the kitchen washed and shaved and drying his hair.*

MARWOOD: Where is he?

WITHNAIL: Sulking up the hill. He says he won't come in for lunch without an apology.

MARWOOD: Suits me. He can eat his fucking radish.

They sit in front of the fire. MARWOOD *cracks a bottle. He's filling the glasses when a voice hisses petulantly in his ear.*

MONTY (*O.S.*): It's all your fault.

MONTY *straightens up with an expression of teasing indignation.*

You lead him astray.

MARWOOD: I beg your pardon, Monty?

MONTY: Oh, don't tell me you're not aware of it. I know what you're up to, and so do you.

WITHNAIL *stands with the bottle. Fills a glass and proffers it.*

Sherry? Oh dear, no, no no. I'd be sucked into his trap. One of us has got to stay on guard. He's so mauve. We don't know what he's planning.

MARWOOD's *expression makes it clear that if* WITHNAIL *participates in this particular tack he will be lunching alone.* WITHNAIL *doesn't participate. And* MARWOOD *escapes into the kitchen.*

81. INT. KITCHEN. COTTAGE. DAY.
Al Bowley scratching in the background. MARWOOD *is at the sink peeling potatoes.* MONTY *joins him at the draining board with his beans. Arse-holed on sherry and enjoying himself.*

MONTY: I'm preparing myself to forgive you . . .

And he closes on him with an intimate whisper.

I think you've been punished enough. (*Smiles*) I think
we'd better release you from the *légumes*, and transfer
your talents to the meat.
Clasping his hand MONTY *heads for the living room.*
MARWOOD *manages to pull away and exchange it for another
nervous smile.*
You shouldn't treat each other so badly. The boy's out here,
frozen to the marrow, and you just sit in here drinking.
MONTY *manoeuvres* MARWOOD *to the fire and re-addresses*
WITHNAIL.
Now come along. He's going to revitalise himself, and
you're going to finish the vegetables.

WITHNAIL: I don't know how to do them.

MONTY: Of course you don't. You're incapable of indulging in
anything but pleasure. Am I not right?
MONTY *misinterprets* MARWOOD's *smile as protection of*
WITHNAIL.
You don't deserve such loyalty.
WITHNAIL *is prised to his feet and escorted into the kitchen.*
Come along. I'm going to teach you how to peel a potato.
MONTY *rolls* WITHNAIL's *sleeves up.* MARWOOD *staring
after them. The geography of the room dislocates through a
slow dissolve.*

82. INT. LIVING ROOM. COTTAGE. DAY.
WITHNAIL *has shaved and they are half-way through lunch.*
MONTY *is going at it with a will. He empties a bottle of wine and
dispatches* WITHNAIL *into the kitchen for a replacement. Despite
a monstrous gobful of food, he manages a smile for* MARWOOD.
*It's reciprocated. Not because he sees anything to smile at. But
because embarrassment forces him to.* MONTY's *stares are hard
enough to itch.* MARWOOD *looks relieved when* WITHNAIL
reappears with a bottle of wine.

MONTY: Isn't it stimulating, getting back to a basic sort of life
for a while?

WITHNAIL: Yes.
His fork plunges into a roast potato almost before he sits down.

MONTY: Surrounded by trees and nature, one feels a glorious
stirring of the senses. A rejection of poisonous inhibition,
and a fecund motion of the soul . . .

MARWOOD: Except of course the problems tend to take the
edge off the pleasure. I mean, with no proper facilities.

MONTY: All the glorious trials of youth. When I was a lad I'd
rocket off on my tandem with Wrigglesworth, and we'd
just ride and ride. And at night, we'd find some barn, and
fall asleep with the perfumes of nature sighing on our skin.
All this said staring at MARWOOD. *He responds with an
awful begummed smile.* WITHNAIL *leans into* MONTY *with
an air of delicacy.*

WITHNAIL: Would it be in bad form to plagiarise a toast?

MONTY: Depends entirely on the quality of the wine. In this
instance, most certainly it would not.
WITHNAIL *tops up the glasses. They raise to the point of
contact.*

WITHNAIL: In that case, to a delightful weekend in the
country.
Both MONTY *and* MARWOOD *are decidedly surprised by the
proposal.* MARWOOD *can't believe his ears and* MONTY
can't believe his luck. He draws MARWOOD *into his pally
conspiracy.*

MONTY: Splendid. We expected a volley of argument . . .
concerning Mr Redgrave!
And here's one of them. MARWOOD'*s voice is as brittle as
glass.*

MARWOOD: You're forgetting Jake, aren't you?

MONTY: Not another word. Jake can wait too.

MARWOOD: Jake isn't a friend, Monty. I hoped to avoid telling
you this, I didn't want to alarm you. But there's a
psychotic on the prowl outside this house.
The news squashes appetite and pleasure. MONTY *turns to*
WITHNAIL.
Ask him whether I exaggerate. He's threatened us, and
he's dangerous.

MONTY: Is this true?

WITHNAIL *lowers his fork. Throws away a light smile. Dilutes it.*

WITHNAIL: Well, there's this local type hanging about. A poacher. Got into a tiff with him, and he threatened me with a dead fish.

His tone proves there are different ways of telling the truth. Yes, it was rather amusing actually. When you came in, we thought it was him. And we thought you scraping your boots was him sharpening his knife.

MONTY: Oh, how delicious . . .

Absolutely fucking hilarious. MARWOOD *can't take any more of this. Fun reverts to feeding.* MONTY *beams across with his utensils poised over the lamb as though about to play a tune on it.*

More meat?

MARWOOD: No thanks. I'm going for some air.

83. EXT. GARDENS. COTTAGE. DAY.

MARWOOD *sits next to the little stream. The sun is setting. The kind of visuals that get into adverts.* WITHNAIL *approaches from the cottage smoking a Turkish cigarette.*

WITHNAIL: I know what you're thinking, but I had no alternative. Old bugger's come a long way, and I didn't wanna put the wind up him.

MARWOOD: Your sensitivity overwhelms me. And if you think you're gonna get a weekend's indulgence up here at his expense, which'll mean him having a weekend's indulgence up here at my expense, you've got another think coming.

WITHNAIL: I give you my word, we'll leave first thing tomorrow morning.

MARWOOD: Tomorrow? Tomorrow? What about *tonight*?

WITHNAIL: He's not gonna try anything . . .

MARWOOD: Of course he is. Why d'you think he's up here? He means business.

WITHNAIL *attempts to lighten the situation. Prevaricating. And concealing it.*

WITHNAIL: Anyway, he sent me out to tell you the coffee's
ready.
MARWOOD: I couldn't drink it. I've got cramp in the mouth
from grinning.
WITHNAIL: Well stop smiling at him.
MARWOOD: I can't help it. I'm so uptight with him, I can't
stop myself.

84. INT. LIVING ROOM. COTTAGE. EVENING.
WITHNAIL *is drinking coffee.* MARWOOD *is staring into his
cup.* MONTY *is arse-holed and on his feet and emoting at the
ceiling.*
MONTY: *Laisse-moi respirer, longtemps longtemps l'odeur de tes
cheveux.* Ah, Baudelaire. Brings back such memories of
Oxford. Oh, Oxford.
The orbs refocus. He heads for the tub with the walking sticks.
Halcyon days. The gentle ego making art. The brutes'
selfishness.

85. EXT. MOUNTAINSIDE. OVER LAKE. EVENING.
A massive panorama with three tiny figures in the far distance.
MARWOOD (*V.O.*): Followed by yet another anecdote about
his sensitive crimes in a punt with a chap called Norman
who had red hair and a book of poetry stained with butter
drips from crumpets.

86. EXT. TRACT. MOUNTAINSIDE. EVENING.
*A pair of field glasses slung round his neck. A walking stick in
his fist. Intoxicated with alcohol. Or the gloaming. Or both.*
MONTY *leads down the track with* WITHNAIL *and* MARWOOD
following.
MONTY: I often wonder where Norman is now. Probably
wintering with his mother in Guildford. A cat and rain.
Vim under the sink. And both bars on.
He turns towards the lake. Hits a sheep with some Latin.
MONTY (*in Latin*): . . . but *old* now . . . *old* . . . There can be
no true beauty without decay.

WITHNAIL (*in Latin*): A requiem for England.

MARWOOD *doesn't understand this. Doesn't like the sound of it.*

MONTY: How right you are. How right you are. We live in a kingdom of rains where royalty comes in gangs. Come on lads, let's get home. The sky's beginning to bruise, night will fall, and we'll be forced to camp.

He takes off down the track. MARWOOD *forcefully detains* WITHNAIL.

MARWOOD: He's having your bed, all right? That's the condition, all right?

WITHNAIL: All right.

MARWOOD: I want the room with the lock. Agree to that, or I'm off.

WITHNAIL: All right. All right.

The cottage emerges from behind a knoll of rock. About sixty yards away. A suspicious figure is moving in the gloom of the gardens. The view stops WITHNAIL *in his tracks.* JAKE *is back. The news is instantly communicated to* MONTY. *Also stops in his tracks. Everyone is concerned. Except* MARWOOD *who's delighted.*

MARWOOD: Good old Jake, eh? I told you, he's back. And that's precisely the reason I'm off to London.

No Old Vic when we feel like it now. WITHNAIL *has the wind up. He stares at* MONTY *who squints through binoculars towards the house.*

Let's all have a good laugh, eh, Withnail? Old Jake's back, eh?

MONTY: He's on his way. He's leaving.

MARWOOD *takes command.* WITHNAIL *and* MONTY *follow him.*

MARWOOD: Come on, let's pack up. We'll get out of here before it gets dark.

87. EXT. COURTYARD. COTTAGE. EVENING.
The gloom thickens. Mostly in MONTY. *They creep the yard and discover a hare hanging on the back door accompanied by a note.*

'Here. Hare. Here. Jake.' *Suddenly everyone is back on holiday.*
Except MARWOOD. *They vanish inside.*

88. INT. BOUDOIR. COTTAGE. NIGHT.
Candlelight and a blazing fire. A good Bordeaux and celery and
Stilton. Ivor Novello singing 'We'll Gather Lilacs' on the
gramophone. This could be 1932.

MARWOOD *looks worried.* WITHNAIL *looks drunk.* MONTY
looks artful. They are playing seven-card-draw poker. Half-crowns
and bottle tops. MONTY *bets from his stack.* MONTY *is*
encouraging WITHNAIL *to drink while* MARWOOD's *glass is filled*
under protest. The only thing he gets from MONTY *is smiles.*
Uptight. No smiles back. There's something going on here. And
MARWOOD *doesn't like the cut of it. Maybe it's imagination but*
WITHNAIL *and* MONTY *seem prepared to giggle for the most*
trivial of reasons. MONTY *deals the cards with a quip for*
MARWOOD's *patently bad hand.*

MONTY (*in Latin*): Looking a bit lonely, isn't he?
WITHNAIL (*in Latin*): He needs a queen to come to the rescue.

> MONTY's *mouth puckers with mirth. A queen for*
> MARWOOD! *It hits like a punch line. Creases* MONTY *and he*
> *and* WITHNAIL *simmer in amusement.* MARWOOD *isn't*
> *amused. Face like a rock. Bets are placed. The room loses*
> *focus via a dissolve.*

89. INT. BOUDOIR. COTTAGE. NIGHT.
MONTY *is cranking at the gramophone. Both the Pernod and*
candles have gone down several inches. A huge stack of beer-bottle
tops and half-crowns in front of WITHNAIL.

He is ferociously drunk. MONTY *returns to the table.*
WITHNAIL's *deal. He can't make it.*

MARWOOD *immediately gets up. Manoeuvres* WITHNAIL *to*
the couch. But the bastard's reneged. Offers resistance. Wants to go
upstairs.

MONTY: I think we'd better get him to bed.
MARWOOD: No, no. He's down here. You're in my room. I'm
in his room. And he's down here.

MONTY: I wouldn't dream of depriving the dear fellow of his
bed. And especially in that condition.
MARWOOD: It's agreed. It's what he wants.
WITHNAIL: No I don't. I wanna get to bed.
And that's precisely where he's heading. Despite MARWOOD's
efforts, he barges for the stairs. MARWOOD *adopts a sort of
instant homosexuality. Dripping wrists and a pink voice.*
MARWOOD: All right then, lovey. Come on. Let's get you to
bed. Early night'll do us good. Night, night, then Monty.
A convoy heads up the stairs. WITHNAIL *gurgles as they
climb.*
WITHNAIL: I wanna be alone. I wanna be alone.

90. INT. TOP OF STAIRS. COTTAGE. NIGHT.
His chances are slim. MARWOOD *has turned into some kind of
nancy boy. The theory is sleep with* WITHNAIL *equals safety. The
landing creaks under* MONTY's *foot.* MARWOOD *has become quite
lovey dovey.*
MARWOOD: Thank you Monty. We're all right now. I've got a
candle in here.
Cradling WITHNAIL *he leads him into the bedroom. Dumps
the vile corpse on his bed.* MONTY's *still at the door as*
MARWOOD *flits out.*
I'll say good night now, Monty.
*He wafts past into his bedroom. Makes the bed in under four
seconds. Grabs items of underwear. Heads back for*
WITHNAIL's *room.*
Huge shadows in the lamplight. MONTY *has just locked
Withnail's door. Key into the pocket. Mr Badger and Mr
Mole.* MARWOOD *is horrified. Instantly an ex-homosexual.*
MONTY *doesn't seem to notice.*
MONTY: I think he'd better sleep alone tonight.
MARWOOD's *mind races. But his feet won't move. He stutters
back.*
He doesn't want to sleep with you.
MARWOOD: All right then. You're in there. I'll get a blanket.
I'll have the couch.

His disappearance into the bedroom is so brief it isn't worth mentioning. He re-appears. Passes MONTY. *Descends the stairs.*

I'll say good night, then.

MONTY: You've already said it. Twice.

He doesn't say it again. Hot foots it through the stairwell door.

91. INT. BOUDOIR. COTTAGE. NIGHT.

MARWOOD *closes the door behind him. It opens again almost instantly.* MONTY *expands into the room. Deals gently with the latch.*

MARWOOD: What is it, Monty? I'm very tired. I need to go to sleep.

MONTY's *fluids are on the move. He glides gently round the room.*

MONTY: But not that tired, eh?

Apparently he is. Starts making his bed up. MONTY *closes on him.*

MONTY: Are you a sponge or a stone?

MARWOOD: What d'you mean?

MONTY: D'you like to experience all facets of life, or do you shut yourself off from new experience?

MARWOOD: I voted Conservative.

MONTY: Are you faithful?

MARWOOD: To whom?

MONTY: Faithfulness isn't selective.

MARWOOD: No, I quite agree. It's more a question of selecting to whom one will be faithful.

MONTY: Have you selected?

MARWOOD: I'm terribly tired.

MONTY: I've been watching you all evening. You've been avoiding my eyes, haven't you?

As off-handedly as possible in reference to these bulbous spheres.

MARWOOD: Your eyes?

MARWOOD's *leg quivers like a gnat's leg in death throes. Tries to articulate but can't.*

MONTY: At luncheon you couldn't take your gaze from mine. This evening you've hardly looked at me.

He's looking at him now. In alarm.

What did he say to you?

MARWOOD: Nothing.

MONTY: You can tell me you know.

MARWOOD: I assure you, nothing. Look here, Monty, I really must go to bed.

MONTY constructs a smile. And then separates it with his tongue.

MONTY: Yes. You must. Mustn't you.

Suddenly his waistcoat is off. Also bow tie.

Off you go then. I shall sleep here. Won't be the first time I've been left with the couch.

MARWOOD wears diving boots to the door. A second later he's gone.

92. INT. BEDROOM. COTTAGE. NIGHT.

All the usual noises of the night. A door banging in the wind. An owl hooting five miles away. A footstep on the bottom stair.

The room is pitch black. Just a hint of light through the window. The footsteps continue to mount. Slow heavy treads. If MARWOOD *is asleep when they begin he's awake by the time they reach his door.*

The door knob turns. A chair holds it for a while. Then fractures slowly under the determination of the intruder. Panic in the dark. He is in. MARWOOD *has no defence other than to pretend to be asleep.*

MONTY: Boy. Boy. I know you're not asleep. Boy.

MONTY moves to the bed. Sits at the end. His voice is quivering.

But he is. I've been into his room. He won't hear a thing.

A key descends on to the bedside table. Owls hooting and snoring.

I know you're not asleep, boy.

MARWOOD: No, I'm not, Monty. What do you want?

He snaps up. A match strikes. A candle lights. Horror. 'Good

God in heaven.' *A huge woman is sitting at the end of the bed.*

MONTY: I had to come. I tried not to. Oh, how I tried not to.
MONTY isn't actually in drag. First glance and the outfit looks like drag. Long paisley silk dressing gown and velvet slippers. Little bit of make up. Nothing ostentatious. A smudge of rouge.

MARWOOD: Look here, Monty. There's something I have to explain to you.

MONTY: You needn't explain. He's told me everything. He told me that first day you came to Chelsea.

MARWOOD: What? What did he tell you?

MONTY: He told me about your arrest in the Tottenham Court Road. He told me about your problems. How you feel. Your desires.

MARWOOD: What problems?

MONTY: You are a toilet trader.

MARWOOD: He told you that?
MONTY somehow manages to motor quickly up the bed on his arse.

MONTY: You mustn't blame him, and you mustn't blame yourself. I know how you feel, and how difficult it is. And that's why you mustn't hold back, ruin your youth as I nearly did over Eric. It's like a tide. Give in to it boy. Go with it. It's society's crime. Not ours.

MARWOOD: I'm not homosexual, Monty.

MONTY: Yes you are. Of course you are. You're simply blackmailing your emotions to avoid the realities of your relationship with him.

MARWOOD: What are you talking about?

MONTY: You love him. And it isn't his fault he cannot love you, any more than it is my fault that I adore you.
That'll do for MARWOOD. He leaps from the bed. Cloaks himself in a blanket and bolts for the door. MONTY is as fast as he is.
Couldn't we allow ourselves just this one moment of indiscretion?

MARWOOD: No.

MONTY: He would never know.

MARWOOD: I don't care what he knows. You've gotta go, Monty. You gotta get out.

He tries to open the door to get out himself. MONTY *isn't having it.* MARWOOD *is inhibited with fear of dropping the blanket. Bit of a scuffle. He rushes across the room with* MONTY *in pursuit. His impassioned voice rises with an overload of emotion.*

MONTY: If you want to humiliate me, humiliate me. I adore you.

MARWOOD *backs off.* MONTY *nails him into a corner. An owl hoots.*

Tell him if you must. I no longer care. I mean to have you . . . even if it must be burglary.

A rapid and almost indecipherable series of protests from MARWOOD. *All to no effect. Not much light to see what's happening. But lips seek lips. A sheer expanse of bosom makes resistance impossible.* MARWOOD *takes what he can. Grabs* MONTY's *ear and screams at him.*

MARWOOD: It's not me. It's him. He lied to you. We're an affair. Have been for years. But he doesn't want you to know. Doesn't want anyone to know.

MONTY *seems to deflate a little.* MARWOOD *still clings to an ear.*

We're both in it. We're obsessed with each other. But he's ashamed. *Ashamed.* He refuses to come out and accept what he is. That's why he's rejecting me while you're here.

The owls hooting. Two naked men in a corner. The bubble bursts.

On my life, Monty. This is the first night we haven't slept together in six years. I can't cheat on him. It would kill him.

MONTY: He told me you were in purgatory because he couldn't love you.

MARWOOD: He's lying. Lying.

A moment later they are retogged in their respective garments.

MONTY: Oh, my boy. Had I know I'd never have attempted to come between you.

MARWOOD: I know that, Monty. I respect you for your sensitivity.

A period of sterile atmospherics. MARWOOD *hastens to the door.*

I thank you for it. But you must leave.

MONTY: Yes. Yes. You'd better go to him.

MARWOOD: I intend to. This instant.

93. INT. BEDROOM. COTTAGE. NIGHT.

The door flies open. MARWOOD *barges in. Y-fronts and an oil lamp.*

MARWOOD: Withnail. You bastard. Wake up.

WITHNAIL'S *forty-a-day tongue hangs from his mouth. Jewelled with a morbid sequin of spittle. His snoring enrages the man in pants.*

Wake up. You bastard. Or I'll burn the fucking bed down.

He moves in with his lamp. A voice muffled with sleep and blankets.

WITHNAIL: I deny all accusations. What do you want?

MARWOOD *grabs his shroud of overcoat and blankets. Wrenches them to the floor.* WITHNAIL *stirs. A waxy body and shotgun revealed.*

MARWOOD: I've just narrowly avoided having a buggering. I've come in here with the express intention of wishing one on you. Having said that, I'm now going to leave for London.

WITHNAIL *regards this threat with enough seriousness to sit up.*

WITHNAIL: Hold on. Don't wanna let your imagination run away with you.

MARWOOD: *Imagination.* I've just finished fighting a naked man. How dare you tell him I'm a toilet trader.

WITHNAIL: It was a tactical necessity.

90

WITHNAIL *scratches his head into focus. Makes an inspection of the candle saucer. Finds a dog end. Lights it. A deep inhalation.*
If I hadn't told him you were active, we'd never have got the cottage.

MARWOOD: I'd never have wanted it. Not with him in it.
A whine of rattling mucus. An evil cough. WITHNAIL *stubs the dog.*

WITHNAIL: God. That hurt. I never thought he'd come all this way.

MARWOOD: *Monty?* He'd go to *New York.*

WITHNAIL: A calculated risk.

MARWOOD: What is all this tactical necessity and calculated risk? This is me naked in a corner. And how *dare* you tell him I love you? And how *dare you* tell him you rejected me?
An almost imperceptible smile stagnates on WITHNAIL*'s mouth.*
How *dare you* tell him that?

WITHNAIL: Sorry about that. I got a bit carried away, sort of said it without thinking.

MARWOOD: Well let me tell you something, Withnail. If he comes into my room again, it's murder.
He grabs the shotgun. Heads for the door. Speaks before the slam.

MARWOOD: And you'll be held responsible in law.

94. EXT. VALLEY. OVER LAKE. DAY.
A big view. Sunlight through thunder clouds. Black edged with gold. Lightning on the horizon. A rumble of thunder. Both it and Crow Crag are several miles away. MARWOOD*'s voice seeps in over the cottage.*

MARWOOD (*V.O.*): . . . and I could not help but hear your unfortunate exchange which I believe was ostensibly caused by me. I do assure you it was not my intention. Nor, may I add, did I expect to bid so empty a valediction as that which circumstances necessitate.

95. INT. LIVING ROOM. COTTAGE. DAY.

WITHNAIL *is up to his elbows in lunch. Cold lamb. Hot potatoes. Plenty of enthusiasm and wine. All in all things have turned out rather well.* MARWOOD *sits opposite reading from Monty's note.*

MARWOOD: Perhaps it is appropriate justice for the eavesdropper that he should leave as his trade determines, in secrecy and in the dead of night. I am, yours ever faithfully. Montague H. Withnail.

An instant of lightning. MARWOOD *crumples the note for the fire.*

Poor old bastard.

WITHNAIL *charges his maw with lamb. Talks through a mouthful.*

WITHNAIL: I would say that that represents a degree of hypocrisy I have hitherto suspected in you but not noticed due to highly evasive skills.

A grand slam of thunder. A moment later it's pissing a monsoon.

MARWOOD: By Christ, Withnail. You'll suffer for this. What you've done will have to be paid for.

WITHNAIL *goes about his grub with a grin. Examines the wine label.*

WITHNAIL: I'll say one thing for Monty. He keeps a sensational cellar.

A toast to Monty is offered. Interrupted by a knock on the door. Infinite possibilities. Has Monty come back?

MARWOOD *walks into the kitchen.* WITHNAIL *staring after him. Opens the back door. A dishevelled* POSTMAN *outside. A telegram handed across.* MARWOOD *closes the door. Opens the envelope. Returns to the living room.* WITHNAIL'S *turn to read the telegram. A smile. Without charity.*

WITHNAIL: Well done.

MARWOOD: Doesn't mean to say I've got it – probably just wanna see me again.

High-voltage lightning.

Well, that settles it then.

WITHNAIL'S *mouth takes a stuffing.* MARWOOD *fights back yawns.*

We're gonna have to leave immediately.

WITHNAIL: What?

MARWOOD: Get your kit together, I'm leaving in half an hour. *And he heads for the stairs, with* WITHNAIL *mouthing after him.*

WITHNAIL: Half an hour? Don't be ridiculous. I need at least an hour for lunch.

96. EXT. MOTORWAY. NIGHT.
Not much traffic about. Thick rain keeps the Jag around seventy.

WITHNAIL (*V.O.*): You got a truck coming up. 'Bout two hundred yards, followed by a slow right hander.

MARWOOD (*V.O.*): I can't keep this up. This is insanity.

97. INT. JAGUAR SEDAN/MOTORWAY. NIGHT.
WITHNAIL *has virtually transferred the dining table to his lap. Here is the leg of lamb. Potatoes. Knife and fork. Bordeaux. And a bottle of gin.* MARWOOD'S *vision is almost entirely obscured. He has to depend on* WITHNAIL *who navigates between mouthfuls.*

WITHNAIL: Stay in this lane. Bear right.

MARWOOD: What lane? I can't see the fucking lane.

WITHNAIL: Bear right. Bear right.
Tail lights of the truck. A near miss. That dreadful sound of a hooter being absorbed by speed. MARWOOD *takes an unnerving.*

MARWOOD: Right. That's it. Next garage I gotta find a windscreen wiper. Plus I gotta get some sleep.
WITHNAIL *doesn't seem concerned. Cackles through a hit of gin.*

98. EXT. MOTORWAY SERVICE AREA. NIGHT.
This is a tourist frightener. A giant boiled egg announces the name of the dump. Not much action. The Jag cruises in looking for the garage section. There isn't one. MARWOOD *pulls over.*

99. INT. JAGUAR/CAR PARK. SERVICE AREA. NIGHT.
MARWOOD *kills the engine. Yawns. Exhausted. Runs hands*

through his hair. WITHNAIL *continues his dinner. Rain batters the roof.*

MARWOOD: Wake me when it stops.

> *He finds pills in the glove compartment. Starts climbing his seat.*

WITHNAIL: What am I supposed to do?

> MARWOOD *gets in the back of the car. Stretches along the seat.*

MARWOOD: Finish your dinner and drop a Surmontil.

> MARWOOD *grabs the gin bottle. Sinks a mouthful to take his pill.*

100. INT. JAGUAR SEDAN/STREETS. WEST LONDON. DAWN.

Mr Hendrix is once again responsible for this music. It cuts to the sequence so brilliantly it is pointless to attempt a description – although one word might help – anarchy.

MARWOOD *is stretched on the back seat. Intermittent patches of orange light wash his face. He wakes slowly. Looks up at the street lights whizzing by. A moment to work it out? Still in the back seat? The car's going like the clappers? But he isn't driving it! Fighting a pill-over he sits and looks over the seat.* WITHNAIL *is at the wheel trying to ram a cripple car!*

But it isn't a cripple car. It's one of those three-wheeled bubble things with a name like a plateful of spaghetti (Isottera?). There's a lot coming into focus at once. (1) WITHNAIL *is drunk. (2) He hasn't got a licence. (3) There's a terrified middle-aged woman in this glass bubble trying to escape. (4) The Jaguar sounds fucked. (5) They're roaring down a slope under the Chiswick flyover.*

MARWOOD: What's going on?

WITHNAIL: I'm trying to ram this bastard.

> MARWOOD *directs eyes at the quarry. She's revving to get away.*

Watch her. Watch her.

MARWOOD: Are you out of your mind? Pull over. You haven't got a licence.

WITHNAIL: No.

Huge close up of the chrome Jaguar. Now it's roaring up a slope and on to the M4. Despite WITHNAIL's *effort the three-wheeler has superior acceleration and pulls away.*

See. We're being overtaken by everything on four wheels. This bastard's aged ten thousand miles in four hundred.

MARWOOD: Where are we?

WITHNAIL: London.

The engine beats like a flabby drum. Firing on only three cylinders. WITHNAIL *floors the accelerator. Forty is about maximum. He hasn't got the mirror together. Turns back over his shoulder.*

Here comes another fucker.

The other fucker pulls alongside. Two faces stare into the Jag. They are both wearing identical hats. They are both POLICEMEN.

MARWOOD: Oh no.

WITHNAIL: It's perfectly all right. Leave them to me.

MARWOOD: You're full of gin you silly tool.

Instructions to pull over are issued. The cops park their van in front of them and get out. As they walk towards the Jag WITHNAIL *hides bottles. A fat face appears at the window.*

WITHNAIL *doesn't open it. A black-leather-clad knuckle taps.* MARWOOD *issues another 'Oh no.' And* WITHNAIL *winds the window down. Nothing is said for a moment. Government eyes scan the bottles. From anyone's point of view this doesn't look good. From a policeman's point of view it looks fucking wonderful. One in the front. Bearded. Clearly drunk. One in the back. Bearded. Clearly drugged.*

POLICEMAN: Bit early in the morning for festivities, isn't it?

WITHNAIL: These aren't mine. They belong to him.

POLICEMAN: You're drunk.

WITHNAIL: I assure you I'm not, Officer. Honestly. I've only had a few ales.

POLICEMAN TWO *examines a front tyre. Sees his reflection in it.*

POLICEMAN: Out of the car. Please. Sir.

101. EXT. CARRIAGEWAY/JAGUAR. SUBURBS. DAWN.

WITHNAIL *and* MARWOOD *get out. All the usual terror. Radios going. Lights flashing. Job satisfaction. Here comes a breath kit.*

POLICEMAN: I want you to take one deep breath, and fill this bag.

> WITHNAIL *looks at the bag. Looks at the copper. Shakes his head.*

POLICEMAN: Are you refusing to fill this bag?

WITHNAIL: I most certainly am.

POLICEMAN: I'm placing you under arrest.

WITHNAIL: Don't be ridiculous. I haven't done anything.

> *The back of the van is opened.* WITHNAIL *is hustled towards it.*

Look here. My cousin's a QC.

> POLICEMAN TWO *turns into a Nazi. Extraordinarily high-pitched.*

POLICEMAN: Get in the back of the van.

> WITHNAIL *gets in the back of the van. Promptly.*
> MARWOOD *joins him.*

102. INT. POLICE STATION. DAY.

A green wall with a cream stripe around it. The room is full of uniforms. WITHNAIL *is handed a sort of bottle and instructed to piss in it. The* ARRESTING OFFICER *escorts him to a corner where he is surrounded with curtains. The sorts of thing that go round hospital beds. Forms are getting filled in at a desk.* MARWOOD *looks at his watch. The constabulary receives tea in mugs.*

These boys are paid to be suspicious. And they are.

POLICEMAN TWO *approaches the curtains. He wants to know if* WITHNAIL *has 'done'. Evidently he hasn't. The curtains are pulled aside and* MARWOOD *gets a view.* WITHNAIL *stares back. Suspicion increases as he turns away. Left arm pumping like a chicken's wing.* MARWOOD *suddenly realises what's happening. The device! The* POLICEMAN *doesn't know what's happening. But knows something is afoot. Pulls his prisoner round. Here's something for the* Police Gazette! *Six inches of transparent plastic tube hang from* WITHNAIL's *zip. A valve on the end of it like a*

*tiny tap. As the cop comprehends what he's staring at this valve
delivers. Now* WITHNAIL's *trying to turn it off. Danny should
stick to dolls.*

103. EXT. STREET. LONDON. DAY.
*A bright sunny day. Cotton wool clouds. Trees in leaf. Flowers. A
luxury new development of apartments. Penthouses at the top. But
all this is to come. Right now the street is dirty and dingy and in the
middle of winter. The Jaguar turns in. Parks opposite the huge
architects' billboard. The only sunny day around here.*

*The warehouse has been demolished. They hardly seem to notice.
Flashing lights all over the pavement. The first wave of wankers
arriving at site. They get out and vanish into their house.*

104. INT. HALLWAY/STAIRWAY. APARTMENT. DAY.
Stagger into the hallway. Utterly wasted. WITHNAIL *makes an
inspection of the mail. A considerable amount of crap. But no
National Assistance payments. This is serious. He looks at*
MARWOOD.

WITHNAIL: Where's our cheques?

MARWOOD: We didn't sign on.

*The house is divided into two apartments. Theirs is on the
upper level.* MARWOOD *unlocks the front door.* WITHNAIL
follows upstairs.

WITHNAIL: That wouldn't make any difference to last week's
payment.

*They've reached the bathroom door. Definitely someone in
there! Half alarmed and half coming-on-brave* MARWOOD
barges in. A vast BLACK MAN *occupies the bath. About three
hundred pounds and as black as your hat.* MARWOOD *looks
at him and he looks back. Nothing said and* MARWOOD *quits
the bathroom and looks at* WITHNAIL. *Still nothing said and*
MARWOOD *is now clattering upstairs. Pushes into a room at
the top.*

105. INT. BEDROOM. APARTMENT. DAY.

Pitch black. MARWOOD *gropes round the bed to get to the window. He tears the curtain apart. An animal on the bed. He jumps back. It's some sort of fox. A moment later a tranquillised man sits up.*

MARWOOD: What are you doing in my bed?

> DANNY *scratches. Mutters something about sleep.*
>
> MARWOOD *is angry.*

MARWOOD: Who's that huge spade in the bath?

DANNY: Presuming Ed.

MARWOOD: All right, you got ten minutes and I want you out . . . 'cause I wanna get in . . . ten minutes, and you better be on your feet.

106. INT. LIVING ROOM. APARTMENT. DAY.

WITHNAIL *is down on the couch with a bottle going.* MARWOOD *has a glass* WITHNAIL *attempts to refill. He refuses it and seems distinctly anxious. Stands and opens the curtains. A stretch in the country and this place is a shock. Smells like a tube station. Air cooked with ashtrays. Just like they left it. The door opens and* DANNY *comes in. Wears his pelt and a school satchel.*

WITHNAIL: How did you get in?

DANNY: Ingenuity, man. Come up the drainpipe.

> DANNY *slings his pelt on the floor. It's a mangy brown fox with glass eyes. A grandmother's garment.*

Would you like a smoke?

WITHNAIL: Yes.

MARWOOD: No thanks. I gotta make a call.

> *He walks to the window, looking at his watch. Evidently still too early.* DANNY *unloads his rolling equipment. A bag of grass and Rizla papers. He begins tearing out a stream of the latter.*

WITHNAIL: What are you gonna do with those?

DANNY: The joint I'm about to roll requires a craftsman. It can utilise up to twelve skins. It is called a Camberwell carrot.

> MARWOOD *turns away from the window.* DANNY *is applying the spittle.*

Withnail and I at the local.

Danny the drug dealer (Ralph Brown) and I.

MARWOOD: It is impossible to use twelve papers on one joint.

DANNY: It's impossible to make a Camberwell carrot with anything less.

WITHNAIL: Who says it's a Camberwell carrot?

DANNY: I do. I invented it in Camberwell and it looks like a carrot.

DANNY introduces WITHNAIL's nostrils to the grass. 'A good bouquet.' The answer is yes. But WITHNAIL's attention is with MARWOOD. He's nervous about his call. And his nerves are making WITHNAIL nervous.

DANNY: D'you realise this gaff's overrun with rodents?

A vibration from outside. MARWOOD gets to his feet again. He looks across the street. A hydraulic hammer is in action on the building site opposite. More wankers are arriving. And DANNY begins to roll.

When I come in I seen one the siza fuckin' dog.

MARWOOD: No, that is a dog. It belongs to the fellow downstairs.

DANNY: Does his dog get in the oven?

MARWOOD: No. His dog doesn't come up here.

DANNY: Then it was a rodent. Opened the oven door, and it was in there lookin' at me. Quite freaked me at the time. I was gonna cook onions.

MARWOOD's watch is getting more attention. Figures it's late enough to make his move. Coat on and he heads for the door.

Are you goin' to bed now?

MARWOOD: No. Phone.

He leaves with WITHNAIL's eyes following. His thoughts are almost visible. A good chance MARWOOD's scored work. What happens then? Doesn't bear thinking about. But he's thinking about it.

DANNY: Who's he gone to telephone?

WITHNAIL: Squat Betty.

He stands and walks to the window. Stares across the street. A phone booth opposite. WITHNAIL's P.O.V. MARWOOD walks inside. WITHNAIL returns to the couch. Swallows wine and clarifies himself.

WITHNAIL: His agent. But he's wasting his time 'cause he
won't be in.

107. INT. (ANOTHER ANGLE). LIVING ROOM.
APARTMENT. DAY.
PRESUMING ED *sits on the sofa. Seeing as he's not saying much
I'm not saying much about him except he's really absolutely huge.
Got a pair of vast 'Loons' on the size of tents. Got a tiny red-leather
beatle cap on top of his big head like a pimple.*

Music – maybe? The Camberwell carrot is completed. DANNY
lights it and fills lungs. A drag or two later it's handed to
WITHNAIL.
DANNY: This'll tend to make you very high.

*This Camberwell carrot represents perfection of the joint
roller's art. An amalgamation of a toilet-roll tube and an
ice-cream cone stuffed with dope.* WITHNAIL *inhales with
respect. Slaps a hand over his mouth to prevent his lungs
rejecting the exhaust.*

This grass is the most powerful in the western
hemisphere. I have it specially flown in from my man in
Mexico. He's an expert. His name's Juan. This grass
grows at exactly two thousand feet above sea level.

MARWOOD *walks in in the middle of this crap. The carrot is
back on its way to* DANNY. *Both look up.* WITHNAIL's *eyes
interrogate. But* DANNY *asks the question.*

Did you get the part, man?
MARWOOD: No.

WITHNAIL's *spirits instantly rise.* DANNY *hands*
MARWOOD *the joint.*
MARWOOD: I got a different one.

MARWOOD *seems in a state of virtual shock. Takes a deep hit
on the joint without much realisation of it. Speaks via a lungful.*
MARWOOD: They want me to play the lead.

A moment of eye contact with WITHNAIL. *Aware of the
potential hurt. But* WITHNAIL *smiles 'Congratulations' and
reaches for the joint.*
DANNY: Where exactly have you two been?

101

MARWOOD: Holiday in the countryside.

DANNY: That's a very good idea. London is a country comin'
down from its trip. We are sixty days from the enda this
decade, and there's gonna be a lota refugees. We're about
to witness the world's biggest hangover, and there's fuck
all Harold Wilson can do about it.

The carrot glows in WITHNAIL's *mouth as he inhales.*

They'll be goin' round this town shoutin' 'Bring out your
dead.'

The joint is handed back to its creator. DANNY *addresses*
MARWOOD.

There was a geezer round here the other day looking for
you.

MARWOOD: What geezer?

DANNY: Some bald geezer. Reckons you owe him two
hundred and sixty six quid back rent. I told him, there's
no questiona payin' rent for a property cut with rodents.

PRESUMING ED *passes the joint to* MARWOOD *who sucks it*
cautiously.

He takes exception to this, and comes on really bald with me.

WITHNAIL: What d'you mean, 'ratty'?

WITHNAIL *has amused himself. Starts to chuckle.* DANNY *is*
serious.

DANNY: I told him to piss off.

A hydraulic hammer starts barking with rabies on the building
site.

MARWOOD: You bloody fool. He'll have us in court again.

DANNY: No he won't. It ain't legal.

WITHNAIL: I assume we can quote you, can we?

WITHNAIL *is still amused.* DANNY *replies with deadly*
sincerity.

DANNY: Law rather appeals to me actually.

WITHNAIL *stares at him. He looks like a stoned sheep. The*
valve of credibility blows in WITHNAIL's *brain. Laughter*
and smoke explode from his face. DANNY *looks at him. Their*
eyes meet. WITHNAIL *falls off the sofa. Rolls hysterically*
with hash giggles.

DANNY *raises a foot to allow him to pass. Retrieves the carrot. Looks towards the raving hysteric at his feet without expression.*

DANNY: Just high.

And so is MARWOOD. *Though he disguises it he isn't enjoying it.*

MARWOOD: Stop laughing. This is serious.

DANNY: No it ain't. I looked into it.

DANNY takes a hit. Offers it to MARWOOD. *This time it's refused.*

I studied the papers.

MARWOOD: What papers?

DANNY: Legal papers.

WITHNAIL *is crying with laughter. Manages enough air to speak.*

WITHNAIL: He can appear for me. And I've got another case pending. He can fight both for me.

Another rictus of laughter. WITHNAIL *tries to crawl away from the table. Fails and falls on his gut.* MARWOOD *is deadly serious.*

MARWOOD: What papers, Danny?

DANNY reaches for his satchel. MARWOOD *grabs it and empties it out on the table. The usual flotsam of food and make up. Also the National Assistance envelopes and a legal-looking document.*

He's got our cheques.

WITHNAIL *is too gone to care. The carrot glows like a log.*

What are you doing with these?

DANNY: I was gonna cash 'em in for ya.

MARWOOD tries to look reasonably at the document. Juan's shipment gets in the way. And so does PRESUMING ED. *He starts spinning* WITHNAIL's *globe with both hands. And chanting to himself with a voice as deep as a well* 'Rama. Rama. Harry Rama . . .'

MARWOOD: For Christ's sake, stop laughing, Withnail. This is a notice of eviction.

PRESUMING ED: Rama. Rama.

WITHNAIL: Give it to my barrister.

PRESUMING ED: Rama. Rama. Harry Rama.

PRESUMING ED's religious ceremony increases the fury of WITHNAIL's hysterics. And heightens MARWOOD's anxiety. He stares at the vast spade spinning Withnail's world around with all the dreadful connotations inherent in it. MARWOOD has gone a proverbial whiter shade of pale. The old black magic is throbbing through his veins. A certain breathlessness is evident. Looks like he's in for a dose.

MARWOOD: Stop laughing. They're thowing us out.

PRESUMING ED: Harry Rama. Harry Rammer. Harry Ramma. Hammy Kalma. Hammy Rammer.

And still the world spins as MARWOOD tries to maintain sanity.

MARWOOD: For God's sake, shut up will you. You're giving me the fear.

He charges the window. Opens it. A warlike blast of pneumatics from the construction site. This is worse. He closes it again.

Gimme a downer, Danny. My brain's capsizing. I've gone and fucked my brain.

DANNY: Change down man. Find your neutral space. You gotta rush. It'll pass. Be seated.

MARWOOD takes his advice. Stares at DANNY with a clenched jaw. The barrister is calmly finishing this huge carrot on his own. Teeth are exposed in a smile. WITHNAIL makes a slow re-entry.

MARWOOD: Aren't you getting absurdly high?

DANNY: Precisely the reason I'm smokin' it.

WITHNAIL: Christ, that was funny.

He crawls back to the sofa. Gets offered the carrot. It's refused.

Couldn't. I'm spaced.

DANNY: Not as spaced as your rodents.

MARWOOD: Don't talk about them.

DANNY: I imagine they're talkin' to each other.

MARWOOD: What d'you mean?

DANNY: I dealt with them.

MARWOOD: Dealt with them. What the fuck d'you mean.

DANNY: Dosed 'em. I expect they're dead down the drain.

Electricity increases voltage. MARWOOD *is losing control again.*

MARWOOD: *Dead down the drain.* What have you done to them?

DANNY: Given 'em all drugged onions.

MARWOOD: *Jesus Christ.* Why have you drugged their onions?

DANNY: Sit down man. Take control.

MARWOOD: Gimme a Valium. I'm getting the fear.

DANNY: You have done something to your brain. You have made it high. If I lay ten mills of Diazepam on you, you will do something else to your brain. You will make it low. Why trust one drug and not the other?

Reality floods on WITHNAIL. *He reaches for the legal document.*

That's politics, isn't it?

MARWOOD: I'm gonna eat some sugar.

And he beetles off into the kitchen with DANNY *speaking after him.*

DANNY: I recommend you smoke some more grass.

MARWOOD (*O.S.*): No way. No fucking way.

DANNY: That is an unfortunate political decision, reflecting these times.

WITHNAIL: What are you talking about, Danny?

DANNY: Politics, man. If you're hanging on to a rising balloon, you're presented with a difficult decision.

The joint has gone out and he relights it and takes a big hit.

Let go before it's too late? Or hang on and keep getting higher? Posing the question, how long can you keep a grip on the rope?.

MARWOOD *returns spooning sugar from a bag. But he doesn't rejoin the group.* WITHNAIL *is no longer smiling. But going down.*

They're selling hippy wigs in Woolworth's man. The greatest decade in the history of mankind is over.

Another lung-shattering hit and he passes the joint to
PRESUMING.

And as Presuming Ed here has so consistently pointed
out, we have failed to paint it black.

108. INT. BEDROOM. APARTMENT. DAY.
*Big close up of an old suitcase on the bed. It's already almost full
and hands stuff the last few items in. The last sock. The last
crumpled shirt. The battered notebook. Written on the cover in
black ink is 'Withnail and I'. The lid of the ancient case is closed
and the catches snapped shut. A hand reaches for a black trilby on
the bed post. The hat journeys across the room and* MARWOOD's
*face is finally revealed. He stares at himself in a mirror. His head
sports a 1914 cut – hard to get used to after such a mane. One thing
he doesn't look is happy. He turns away. Rain is drumming on the
window. What few possessions he has are packed in cardboard
boxes. He picks up his case and pauses at the door. A last look
around the room he knows he'll never see again.*

109. INT. LIVING ROOM. APARTMENT. DAY.
WITHNAIL *looks up from the sofa as* MARWOOD *walks in.
Nothing said because there isn't much to say. But the eyes are
saying a lot. Both are aware this is it. It is time to say goodbye.*
MARWOOD: My dad'll pick up the boxes in the week, and he's
     gonna do something about the car.
     WITHNAIL *nods and smiles a bit. And* MARWOOD *smiles a
     bit back.*
     Well, I'm off now, then.
WITHNAIL: Already?
     *And he suddenly animates and is gonna make it harder than it
     is.*
     I've got us a bottle open.
     He flourishes it with great glee. MARWOOD *clearly wants to
     leave.*
     I confiscated it from Monty's supplies. Fifty-three
     Margaux, best of the century. I'm sure he wouldn't resent
     us a parting drink.

He's about to fill a pair of waiting glasses. But MARWOOD *doesn't want to wait. Wants the goodbye over with and wants out of here.*

MARWOOD: I can't Withnail. I've gotta walk to the station. I'll be late.

WITHNAIL: There's always time for a glass.

MARWOOD: No. I don't have the time.

WITHNAIL: All right. I'll walk you through the park, we can drink it on the way.

The last thing MARWOOD *wanted to hear. But* WITHNAIL *is already climbing into his overcoat and scarf and grabs his brolly to leave.*

110. EXT. REGENT'S PARK. CAMDEN TOWN. DAY.
The park is as bleak and deserted as it's ever been. The afternoon is dissolving into threadbare rain. They walk the paths like they've done a dozen times before. But they were together then. And now they're already alone. Strangers already. And the sweet and sour music is but an addition to the wider sentiment.

MARWOOD *carries his battered suitcase.* WITHNAIL *his battered black umbrella. His bottle is half drunk and he attempts to hand it over again. But this time* MARWOOD *shakes his head.*

MARWOOD: No. No more, thanks.

So WITHNAIL *drinks another mouthful.* MARWOOD *is almost in pain.*

Listen, Withnail. It's a stinker. Why don't you go back?

WITHNAIL: Because I wanna walk you to the station.

MARWOOD: Well, don't. Please, don't.

They stop and stare at each other. Just the sound of rain beating on the umbrella . . .

I really don't want you to.

The vacuum has been burst and there's a lot of silence about.

MARWOOD *lays a hand on his friend's shoulder. Almost a whisper.*

I shall miss you, Withnail.

And the sadness has finally hit and WITHNAIL *is looking bleak.*

WITHNAIL: I shall miss you too. Chin-chin.

He offers a toast and drinks and MARWOOD *turns and walks away.* WITHNAIL *watches him evaporate into rain. He doesn't look back.*

Just the sound of rain beating on the umbrella.

WITHNAIL *walks a little way with his bottle and almost inadvertently finds himself in front of the wolves' cage. He hangs wrists over the railings staring at the pissed-off wolves. They stare back looking as sad as him. He addresses one with a profound lack of sentiment.*

I have of late, but wherefore I know not, lost all my mirth.

And the fifty-three again journeys to his lips. The wolf keeps staring. WITHNAIL *keeps speaking like a natural instinct.*

And indeed, it goes so heavily with my disposition, that this goodly frame the earth, seems to me a sterile promontory.

Now the wine is adding some volume. This is WITHNAIL *back in gear. And all his pride and rage is adding emotion.*

This most excellent canopy the air, look you, this brave o'erhanging firmament, this majestical roof fretted with golden fire, why it appeareth nothing to me but a foul and pestilent congregation of vapours.

WITHNAIL *is suddenly on a stage somewhere. Obviously at Stratford. And his expression asks: And by God, I'd be good enough, wouldn't I? Absolutely brilliant, wouldn't I? No more sadness now. All the fire is back. And all the power!*

What a piece of work is a man, how noble in reason, how infinite in faculties, how like an angel in apprehension, how like a god.

He looks at the wolves in wonder that the bastards aren't clapping.

The beauty of the world; the paragon of animals; and yet to me, what is this quintessence of dust? Man delights not me, no, nor women, neither . . . nor women neither.

Albert Finney never felt so good. He takes a last and final slug at the bottle and casts it aside. By Christ, that was the best rendition of Hamlet the world will ever see! The only pity was

it was only wolves that saw it. They stare at WITHNAIL
*through the bars. He bids them a silent good afternoon and
walks away.*

  *P.O.V. wolves..*WITHNAIL *walks across the park until
he is a tiny figure in the distance. The sweet and sour music
rises into appropriate orchestral perfection as he finally, and
far away, disappears.*

How to Get Ahead
in Advertising

And did those feet in ancient time
Walk upon England's mountains green?
And was the holy Lamb of God
On England's pleasant pastures seen?

And did the Countenance Divine
Shine forth upon our clouded hills?
And was Jerusalem builded here
Among these dark Satanic Mills?

Bring me my bow of burning gold!
Bring me my arrows of desire!
Bring me my spear! O clouds, unfold!
Bring me my chariot of fire.

I will not cease from mental fight,
Nor shall my sword sleep in my hand
Till we have built Jerusalem
In England's green and pleasant land.

William Blake, 1804–8

Would to God that all the Lord's people were prophets.

Numbers, 11:29

1. INT. CONFERENCE/SCREENING ROOM. ADVERTISING
AGENCY.
*An oblong room with a twenty-seat conference table. About four of
the chairs are occupied. Four men and one woman all in their early
twenties. The room is in semi-darkness and fretted with cigarette
smoke. At one end an image is projected on to a small screen. It is of
a pretty blonde exiting from a supermarket. She embraces a pair of
grocery sacks spilling over with fresh vegetables.*

Caption

You might have to go a little out of your way for our
participating stores – when you do, you'll find we've gone out
of our way for you.

> *A figure paces at the end of the room. Suffering a smoker's
> cough. He wears shirt sleeves and red braces. He carries a
> china coffee cup and saucer which chinks occasionally as he
> drinks. He walks in and out of the image. But is not
> recognisable until he stops in the middle of it. The girl
> superimposes across* BAGLEY's *face.*

BAGLEY: Let me try and clarify some of this for you. Best
Company Supermarkets are *not* interested in selling
'wholesome foods'.
*Although he isn't actually drunk it's clear he has been
drinking.*
They are not worried about the nation's health. What *is*
concerning them, is that the *nation* appears to be getting
worried about its health. And *that* is what is worrying Best
Co.

117

And he disappears into the shadows and a cigarette lighter clicks.

Because Best Co wants to go on selling them what it always has: i.e. the white breads, baked beans, canned foods, and that suppurating, fat-squirting, little heart attack traditionally known as the British sausage.

He moves back into the light filling the projection beam with a lungful. Hard to focus on what but there's something disturbing about him. And it hasn't gone unnoticed by the junior copywriters.

So, how can we help them with that? Clearly, we are looking for a label. We need a label brimming with health. And everything from a Nosh Pot to a white sliced will wear one with pride. And although I'm aware of the difficulties of coming to terms with this, it must be appreciated from the beginning, that even the Nosh Pot must be *low* in something, and if it isn't, then it must be *high* in something else! And that is its 'health-giving ingredient' we will sell.

Eyes meet across the table. Is Bagley OK? He sounds almost manic.

BAGLEY: Which brings me to my final question. Who are we trying to sell this to? *Answer.* We are trying to sell it to the archetypal, average housewife. *She who fills her basket.* What you have here is a twenty-two-year-old pretty girl, and what you need is a taut slob. Something on Foot Deodorisers in a brassière.

After a suitable silence a young man in a bow tie decides to speak. He gestures to a heap of documents. The accent is broad Liverpool.

JUNIOR COPYWRITER: I'm not sure we can go along with that, Mister Bagley. If you look at the market research . . .

BAGLEY *dismisses his research. From now on the volume is going up.*

BAGLEY: I don't need to look at the market research. I've lived with thirteen and a half million housewives for fifteen years! And I can tell you everything about them. She is thirty-seven years old. She has two point three children, one point six of which will be girls. She uses sixteen feet six inches of toilet tissue a week, and fucks no more than four point two times a month. She's got seven radiators and is worried about her weight, which is why we have her on a diet. And because we have her on a diet, we also encourage her to 'reward herself' with little 'treats'. And she deserves them. 'Cause anyone existing on twelve hundred calories of artificial, synthetic, orange-flavoured waffle a day deserves a little treat. We know it's naughty, but you *do* deserve it. Go on darling, *swallow a bun!* And she does. And the instant she does, the guilt cuts in, and so here we are again with our diet! It's a vicious, but quite wonderful circle. And it adheres to only *one* rule. Whatever it is, *sell it*. And if you wanna stay in advertising, by God you'd better learn that.

2. INT. CORRIDOR/SPIRAL STAIRCASE. AGENCY. DAY.
This agency looks like an advert for itself. Ebony-coloured glass and super-efficient-looking chrome. BAGLEY *foots it quickly along a corridor. Coughing lightly between deep inhalations on a cigarette. He passes an open office door and gets just what he does not want. A porky art director scuttles out and* BAGLEY *attempts to ignore him.*

RICHARD: Bagley, it is not in my nature to be a pain in the ass with such consistency. It's being forced upon me. I just had them on the phone again, they're calling back in five minutes and I've gotta give them something.

BAGLEY: Just tell 'em it's gonna be wonderful. (*A passing face.*) Hi, Harry . . .
    BAGLEY *descends a spiral glass staircase with the* ART DIRECTOR *following.*

RICHARD: I've told them that, and they're over the moon (and apart from fifteen calls a day wondering where the fuck it is) they couldn't be happier. They're getting impatient. *And now they arrive in a corridor. The* ART DIRECTOR *continues to chew it.*

119

We promised them the animatic over a week ago, and I'll
be frank with you, Bagley, I'm running out of bullshit.

BAGLEY: Try massaging your temples . . .

RICHARD: I've got to give them a *date*. Either a date, or you've
got to give me some idea of what you're coming up with.

BAGLEY: I'm coming up with a brilliant advertisement for a
very dull pimple cream.

RICHARD: Then why can't I take a look?

He follows into a small office. A SECRETARY *hammers a
typewriter.*

Why can't I see something? Just a storyboard, or some
roughs. Anything, so I can give them an idea of the
direction you're going in.

BAGLEY: No. I don't show work in progress. (*To*
SECRETARY) Any calls?

MAUD: Mr Bristol called again. Twice.

BAGLEY: I hope you told him I was out.

MAUD: Yes, Mr Bagley. You *were* out.

BAGLEY: Good, and if he calls again, I'm still out.

RICHARD: Bagley, you gotta give me a date.

BAGLEY: All right, try a Monday on 'em. And don't get so
panicky. Nobody ever remembers a late delivery,
Richard, they only ever remember a bad one.

*He barges through an inner door. Slams it hard as he
disappears.*

3. INT. STUDIO/OFFICE. ADVERTISING AGENCY. DAY.
*Probably the most luxurious office in the building. Cinemascope
windows with a panoramic over the Thames. The Houses of
Parliament are visible in the distance. An antique telescope stands
in front of the view. Everything else is high-quality hi-tech. Two
TV screens and a word-processor. Next to the desk is a bright-red
household trash can. There are also dozens and dozens of awards.*

*Every space and surface carries some visual testament to
Bagley's success. Gold discs and posters. Everything in here is
designed to produce commercials. And the only thing out of place is*
BAGLEY.

*Until further notice he will be smoking perpetually. He's
smoking now. He's also pacing up and down with a kind of
anxiety-induced static in his eyes. He stops occasionally. Lips
moving like a demented attempting to follow some internal
conversation. Now he's off again at speed. Snapping his fingers
together. Dragging fingers through his hair. He's staring at the
ceiling. He's staring at the floor. Littered with discarded ideas. He
is seeking some kind of inspiration. Clearly got a problem with the
pimple cream.*

*And now he's looking through the telescope to see if there's any
hope of an idea out there. He scans the river muttering all the time.
Now he's trying an aggressive tone.* 'THE BOIL BUSTERS! Your
face can be a battle-ground. You need something tough!'
*Forget it. Forget it. Nothing. (A snap insert of Big Ben. It's four
ten p.m.)*

BAGLEY (*V.O.*): What do they want another pimple cream for?
The market's saturated.

BRISTOL (*V.O.*): There's a lotta boils out there, Bagley.

BAGLEY *is on the move again. Flips on his video. Gets a still
of a youth with acne. Kisser like half a Stilton. Too much to
bear he turns away lighting another cigarette. He's already got
one burning in a saucer on the other side of the room. He
forgets the one in his face. Retraces his steps and arrives back
at his saucer. Inadvertently picks up the cigarette. There are
now two in his mouth. He wouldn't know if there were fifty.
Because a ghost of a dissolving idea stops him in his tracks. It
manifests as a sincere American.*

BAGLEY: Nobody cares as much about your skin as you do.
But we do try. And because we care, we went to an expert,
Mother Nature. And we discovered that sometimes the
most effective way of dealing with those troublesome little
breakouts is Mother Nature's own, richest source of
vitamin A. So we took essential oils of carrot, marigold
seed, roots and other natural 'ingredients' . . . (*Now he's
losing it.*) And we packed this shit into every tube.
*And now he's lost it. Also lost the accent. Almost lost his
temper.*

121

We called it H/P 'Mega-Veg'. And if it doesn't work on your blackheads, you can spread the fucker on toast!
Cynicism powers him back to reality. For a moment he looks insane. MAUD *enters with reluctance. And is reluctant to pass on the news.*

MAUD: Sorry to disturb you, Mr Bagley, but Mr Bristol's on the line again . . .

BAGLEY: Well tell him I'm out again.

MAUD: He says he knows you're not. He says he knows you're avoiding him. And he says he insists on a time to see you.
BAGLEY *grasps at his hair as though he's just about to shampoo it.*

BAGLEY: For Christ's sake, gimme a break! All right, tell him tomorrow. This time tomorrow. And get my wife on the phone.
MAUD *leaves to go about it and* BAGLEY *produces a bottle of booze.*
Acne? What the fuck rhymes with *acne*? Back me, pack me, sack me.
He pours a large slug of whisky. Downs it in one and gets a click! Here comes a huge artificial smile and a sexy strut up the carpet.

BAGLEY: Hi, my name's Barbara Simmonds, and I'm a biochemist. But at night I'm a woman. And I want my skin to be at its best. So I recommend a new product. It's called (whatever the fuck it's called) and I use (whatever the fuck it is) because I *know* it works. And *I* should know. Because *I* make it.
He stops and stares into space. Something's coming. Yes. *He's getting something. The eyes are widening. Something's definitely com . . .*

MAUD (*via intercom*): Mrs Bagley on line one.
It shatters like a house of cards. And BAGLEY *throttles the phone.*

BAGLEY (*into phone*): What d'you want!
Apparently she wants to know what he wants because he called her.

Yes, I'm sorry, darling, of course I did. Listen, I don't think I'm gonna get back tonight. I'm gonna blitz it. No, fine, fine, it's going fine. It's just that the deadline's getting serious. Really? Well we could meet for lunch? Celebrate my breakthrough. OK, one o'clock. I'm not totally sure yet, but I think I'm going 'Medical' . . .

4. INT. STUDIO/OFFICE. ADVERTISING AGENCY. NIGHT.

BAGLEY *stares into a mirror on his wall. On the coast of drunkenness now. He swills the last few inches of Scotch from the bottle. Considerable degeneration has taken place. The eyes are par-boiled and livid. The tongue is poached. And there's an intermittent flat-battery cough. His collar hangs on a single stud. The braces are down like huge bra straps. He's beginning to look like Garth.*

BAGLEY (*V.O.*): We wanted to be as honest with you as your mirror. So many products will tell you bare-faced lies, but we know you can't lie with a bare face. So we didn't hire any fancy ad-men to fool you with their fancy words. We didn't even give it a fancy name . . .

And off he goes round the office taking hits of his Scotch.

BAGLEY (*V.O.*): We simply called it . . .

His travels have taken him to the telescope and he looks through.

BAGLEY (*end V.O.*): Five A.M. 'Cause that's the time it was discovered. For God's sake, gimme a line. Gimme a line. *Big Ben strikes five to prove it. He lobs the dead bottle at his bin.*

. . . so we added 'Nature's own natural moisturisers'. What *are* 'Nature's own, added, natural moisturisers'? *The question momentarily freezes him. He answers it with contempt.*

Water. We added, water. D'you wanna buy it? It's got *real* water in it.

Clearly arrived at the point where he hates the produce and market.

We added *real rain* made of water. *T.M.*

123

*The 'T.M.' is added to the sentence with a tone of utter
loathing. And something terrible's just happened. He's run out
of cigarettes. Suddenly he's on hands and knees in his red
dustbin looking for a butt. Hundreds of 'anxiety balls' spill
across the carpet. Here are dozens and dozens of rejected ideas
in gristles of crumpled paper.*

*BAGLEY is looking for a suitable dog-end and finds several
quickly. Lights up and realises he's still looking for an idea.
He begins unravelling the balls of paper. Maybe some of these
aren't so bad after all? 'The Pimple Pen?' No. Forget it. 'Fat
Suckers?' Forget it! But what's this? 'Hi, My name's
Barbara Simmonds.' This isn't bad. He lights one dog from
the other. Straightens the paper out. Rises to his knees and
manages to come up with an American accent.*

BAGLEY: Hi, my name's Barbara Simmonds, and I'm a
biochemist. But at night . . . when I'm home, with
everything off . . .
*He thinks hard. Very very hard. And all he can come up with
is*
I'm a naked bio-chemist . . .
*The Barbara Simmonds pitch is screwed into a ball for the
second time. With an expression of awe-inspiring desolation he
crawls towards a bathroom. He stands with the assistance of
the door-knob and goes inside. Fatigue has won this one.
There's no other way but a pill.*

*He opens a bathroom cabinet and shuffles through a mass
of bottles. Valium is the only answer. He shakes a pair out
and swallows them without water. Leans on the sink with
hands either side.*
I gotta get something. I just gotta get *something*!
*So he has one last try. Fighting the booze he produces one last
desperate ruptured smile.*

BAGLEY: Hi, my name's Bio Simmonds, and I'm a Barbara
chemist . . . Oh, for God's sake . . . Jesus, God, give me a
break.
*Almost laughing with desperation his forehead greets the taps.
He stands again and closes the bathroom cabinet. For half a*

split second he sees a horrible *face reflected behind him. This is Catherine Deneuve in* Repulsion. *Except unlike Catherine* BAGLEY *screams out.*

Ahhhh!!! . . . Who the fuck are you?

He's faced by a dreadful-looking little female Greek dwarf with a badly plucked moustache. She sports a brush and bucket and a mop.

GREEK DWARF: I am cleaner. Me.

That'll do for BAGLEY *and he staggers out hoping for some sleep.*

5. INT. 'CLOUDS' ITALIAN RESTAURANT. DAY.

The walls are white and the art is modern. It's a snazzy Italian joint. Ashtrays changed twice a minute whether it's necessary or not. In this case it's necessary. BAGLEY *is lighting another. His wife sits opposite. Late twenties and beautiful. Her name is* JULIA.

JULIA: You're chain-smoking, darling.

BAGLEY: I know I am . . . I know I am.

A WAITER *arrives with a pair of menus.* BAGLEY *finishes his drink.*

I'd like another vodka martini. Dry as a bone, twist, no olive.

JULIA: Spritzer, please.

BAGLEY: I tell you, Julia, I'm outta my mind. I'm getting nowhere. Zero.

JULIA: Stop getting so wound up about it. It'll come. And please put that cigarette out. That's three in ten minutes.

BAGLEY *reluctantly obliges. Looks in the very bowels of suffering.*

JULIA: Dar-ling . . . why don't you forget it a minute? Take the afternoon off.

BAGLEY: I can't . . . I gotta see Bristol.

JULIA: Well, you're not gonna be much use.

BAGLEY: That's where you're wrong, Julia. That's what's so insane about all this. Anything else I'm fine. Gimme any other part of the human body and I'll sell it something.

Gimme a bald head, and I'll sell it shampoo. But I cannot get a handle on the boils.

JULIA: Would you pass the butter, darling?

BAGLEY: The moment I think of a boil, my mind slips into a sort of dreadful, oily neutral. I just sit there, hour after hour, chewing the ends off pencils, smoking myself daft.

JULIA: What exactly is this stuff?

BAGLEY: It's a standard sixteen to twenty-six-year-old 'acne attacker'. It's a hexafluoride.

JULIA: Does it work?

BAGLEY: I've no idea. It's probably junk.

JULIA: And that's probably the problem. If you knew it worked, actually got rid of boils, you'd probably have no problem selling it.

BAGLEY: Nobody in advertising wants to get rid of boils, Julia – they're good little money spinners. All we wanna do is offer *hope* of getting rid of them. And that's where I'm blocked.

He interrupts himself to ask a passing WAITER

Where's our drinks?

WAITER: Coming, sir.

JULIA: I really do think you should cancel Bristol, and come home with me.

BAGLEY: Can't, I been cancelling him all week. Why can't we cancel this dinner? I'm not in the mood for that mob. If I'd known we were having dinner, I'd never have suggested lunch.

JULIA: We can have both. People do, darling.

BAGLEY: I suppose Wheelstock'll be there?

JULIA: Don't start taking it out on Penny . . .

The drinks arrive simultaneously with a middle-aged COUPLE *at an adjacent table. These two are a bit on the 'tweedy' side. Corgi's outside in the Jag. They're instantly aware of* BAGLEY *and it would be hard not to be. He goes for his cocktail and downs it in one. A whispered protest from* JULIA *is drowned in a fit of coughing. Between the rasps* BAGLEY *articulates.*

BAGLEY: Oh Christ, what am I gonna do?

JULIA: Dennis, for goodness sake, stop getting so paranoid. Everything'll be all right. You've had these sort of problems many, many times before.

BAGLEY: Not like this I haven't.

There now follows one of those horribly intense conversations that nobody is meant to hear but everybody in the area is listening to.

JULIA: Oh yes you have. What about *piles*? You had a terrible time with piles.

BAGLEY: I did *not* have a terrible time with piles. All right, I may have had a problem getting a hold on them, but selling them was a piece of cake.

JULIA catches the eyes of the middle-aged COUPLE next to them. Coming out of context these old buggers are astonished by the exchange.

JULIA: You're raising your voice, darling.

BAGLEY: Compared to this, piles were a birthday present. So was dandruff. So was breath.

JULIA: You're still raising your voice, darling.

BAGLEY: I can tell you, Julia. The whole lot taken together, including the fucking lawnmowers, *is as nothing* compared to the pimples, acne and boils.

A WAITER arrives to take orders and JULIA smiles out of the vacuum.

JULIA: I think I'll have crab mousse, followed by a Dover sole. You, darling?

BAGLEY: Nothing. I couldn't eat a thing.

WAITER: We have very nice linguini today.

BAGLEY: No thank you. I've got absolutely no appetite. Probably due to the vast amount of wood I'm eating.

That settles it for the OLD BOY. He's about to ask to move tables.

JULIA: I don't think I'm that hungry myself. I'm sorry, would you just bring us the bill for our drinks?

6. EXT. WESTMINSTER BRIDGE. EMBANKMENT. DAY.
*A black Range Rover with tinted windows crosses the bridge. Pulls
up outside a tower block.* BAGLEY *gets out of the passenger door
and walks round to the driver's side. He's looking at the building.
Also looking very ill at ease. His wife puts on a brave face for him.*
BAGLEY: I don't wanna go back in there.
JULIA: Don't worry about it. Don't think about boils. If a boil
    pops up, force yourself to think of something else.
BAGLEY: OK.
JULIA: And don't go anywhere near your office. Just see
    Bristol and come home.
BAGLEY: Are you sure you can't wait for me?
    *No unfortunately she can't. She kisses him and melts into the
    traffic.*

7. INT. ELEVATOR. TOWER BLOCK.
BAGLEY *is looking at the floor numbers. Floor three and the
elevator stops. Doors open and a young* GIRL *walks in. Doors close
and we are back on our way.* BAGLEY *quickly becomes aware of a
big boil on the side of this* GIRL's *nose. It's the last thing he wanted
to see. But he's forced to stare at it. Captivated by this potent
feruncle.*
    *Equally quickly she becomes aware of his interest. Their eyes
meet and he tries a smile. It manifests as a horrible ingratiating
grin. Who is this fucker? Some kind of rapist? They're both pleased
when the lift reaches floor seventeen and* BAGLEY *shunts into his
agency.*

8. INT. RECEPTION. ADVERTISING AGENCY. DAY.
*The reception area is like the foyer of a huge 1930s cinema. A
peroxided* BLONDE *works the desk.* BAGLEY *passes issuing an
instruction.*
BAGLEY: Get Bristol on the line. Tell him I'm coming in to see
    him now.
    He vanishes up the spiral stairs. The RECEPTIONIST *makes
    the call.*

9. INT. OFFICE. ADVERTISING AGENCY. DAY.

Similar in size to Bagley's office and also looking over the river. At present so is BAGLEY. *He patrols up and down in front of the windows. Occasionally activates any one of a number of executive toys. A row of ridiculous ball bearings bash into each other.*

He turns as BRISTOL *walks in. Several things to mention about him. First he is as bald as a coot. Going through a sort of puberty in reverse. Apart from the eyebrows there is hardly any facial hair at all. Second he's fifty-five and overweight. And third he wears a remote-phone head-set that keeps him in touch with the outside world. It's like a light-weight Walkman. Tiny earphones with a transparent tube in front of the mouth. What makes it absurd on Bristol's naked pate is the ten-inch aerial waggling above his left ear.*

This is for the serious telephone user. During the scene he'll occasionally transmit and receive. Conversation will be (in brackets).

BRISTOL: Sorry to keep you waiting, Bagley. Didn't expect you till four o'clock.

He bustles past with a grin and hands BAGLEY *a coloured photostat.*

Here. Take a look at this.

BAGLEY: What is it?

BRISTOL: It's a photostat of an ass on a copying machine. Don't recognise it do you?

BAGLEY: Not offhand, no.

It seems to amuse BRISTOL. 'Dirty little tart.' *He gestures* BAGLEY *to a seat that's declined. Starts stuffing a pipe with tobacco.*

BRISTOL: Hear you gave the juniors a bit of a tongue lashing yesterday.

BAGLEY: Really?

BRISTOL: Said you went over the top.

BAGLEY: I haven't got time to give lessons in advertising. They asked my opinion and I gave it. And in my opinion they'd completely missed the brief.

BRISTOL walks away from his desk filling the atmosphere with smoke.

BRISTOL: Mmm . . . mmm . . . I think you're probably right. (Not now, Sheila.) As a matter of fact I think you helped them out. (About fifteen minutes.) Anyway, that's not actually what I wanted to talk about . . .

BAGLEY *suppresses his anxiety aware of what he wants to talk about.*

How we getting on with the pimple cream?

BAGLEY *wings it and manages to come up with a confident response.*

BAGLEY: Five minutes.

BRISTOL: Is it special? (227 0472)

BAGLEY: *Sensational.*

BRISTOL: Can you give me a verbal peek?

BAGLEY: You know me, John. I'd rather not.

BRISTOL: That's what I thought. And I'm very pleased to hear it (no, *Los Angeles*, 227 0472) 'cause I'll tell you frankly, Bagley, they were on the phone this morning threatening to pull the account. Anyone but you and they would.

BAGLEY *smiles basking in the brilliance he knows he no longer has.*

BAGLEY: It's finished – just a fine tune. I'll be through over the weekend.

BRISTOL: Can we diarise on that?

BAGLEY: Of course.

BRISTOL: Wonderful. Wonderful. (Yes, put him through . . . mmm-hum . . . mmm-hum, really? Why so fast? *Really*?)

BRISTOL *is smiling now. Moving round the office. Puffing his pipe.*

(What happened to Seymour, Hick, Washbone, Riddle and Gore? . . . Really? Ha! Ha! Ha, ha, ha! . . . What about S and S? Ha, ha! . . . What is it a kipper? Oh, that's interesting . . . what, a complete range of dinners? All frozen fish?)

BRISTOL *activates a little spiral of penguins. They climb a plastic mountain. Whizz down again.* BAGLEY *is on his way to the door.*

Just hold on a second, Bagley. (No, he's here now. I'll ask

him . . . No, no, he's finished, he'll be through Monday
for sure . . . Wait a sec, Eddie.)

BRISTOL *sticks a forefinger over his tube. Looks across at*
BAGLEY.

BRISTOL: Can you handle a Monday pitch? It's a quickie,
you'll have to go in dry.

BAGLEY: What's the product?

BRISTOL: It's a 'Boil in a Bag'?

The concept roots BAGLEY *to the spot. Bad electricity in his
eyes.*

BRISTOL: Are you all right, Bagley?

BAGLEY: Yes, I'm fine. Tell him OK I'll be in first thing,
Monday morning.

10. INT. COMPARTMENT. COMMUTER TRAIN. EVENING.
A first-class-filthy example of a British Rail compartment.
BAGLEY *sits close up in a corner. His eyes are closed but he isn't
asleep. Once again his lips are imperceptibly moving. It's a stale
internal conversation. Obviously boils still weigh heavily on his
mind.*

JULIA (*V.O.*): You must stop worrying. If a boil pops up,
force yourself to think of something else.

BAGLEY (*V.O.*): You're absolutely right. I'm absolutely not
gonna think about boils. Large boils . . . blind boils . . .
or fat girls' boils till ten o'clock tomorrow morning.

His eyes close tight in agreement. But his brain is still on fire.
How about large – blind – fat girls – with boils?

*And he snaps forward like somebody forcing himself out of a
nightmare. He's surprised to see five eyes staring back at him.
The first four belong to a pair of* BUSINESSMEN. *The other is
the property of a swarthy* PRIEST *with a flesh-coloured
eye-patch to go with it.*

*There is a brief embarrassed silence before all eyes avert.
The businessmen's into newspapers and the* PRIEST's *up into
the luggage rack.*

BALD BUSINESSMAN: I see the police have made another
lightning raid. 'Paddington Drug Orgy.'

NOT BALD BUSINESSMAN *grunts dismissively but the*
PRIEST *wants to get into conversation. He speaks with a*
heavily ingrained Northern Irish brogue.

PRIEST: I'd birch the lot of 'em. Birch 'em. Give 'em
something to fear. It's the only way to put a stop to it.
A pack of Sweet Afton comes out. Offered to and refused by
BALD BUSINESSMAN.

PRIEST: I suppose there was young girls involved?

BALD BUSINESSMAN: One discovered naked in the kitchen,
'breasts smeared with peanut butter'.
Increasing the PRIEST'*s interest.* BALD BUSINESSMAN
continues reading it out.
Police took away a bag containing fifteen grams of
cannabis resin, it may also have contained a quantity of
heroin.
BAGLEY *is about to focus on the most important item in his*
life.

BAGLEY: Or a pork pie.
All five eyes snap in his direction. BAGLEY *stares back with*
an expression of reciprocal surprise. It is as though someone
else has said it. But it seems this pie has driven like a
thunderbolt through his confusion and for the first time he
appears to relax.

BALD BUSINESSMAN: I beg your pardon?

BAGLEY: I said the bag may also have contained a pork pie.

BALD BUSINESSMAN: I hardly see a pork pie's got anything to
do with it.
And neither did NOT BALD BUSINESSMAN. *Neither did the*
PRIEST. BAGLEY *almost smiles.*

BAGLEY: All right then, what about a large turnip? It may also
have contained a big turnip?
It's obvious nobody considers a big turnip an acceptable
alternative to a pork pie. After a space of silence the PRIEST
settles it.

PRIEST: The bag was full of drugs.

BAGLEY: Nonsense.

PRIEST: The bag was full of drugs. It says so.

And he would have taken the Express *to prove it were it not resisted.*

BAGLEY: The bag could have been full of anything. Pork pies. Turnips. Oven parts. It's the oldest trick in the book.

PRIEST: What book?

BAGLEY: The distortion of truth by association book. The word is *may*. You all believe heroin was in the bag, because cannabis resin was in the bag. The bag *may* have contained heroin, but the odds are one hundred to one certain that it didn't.

BALD BUSINESSMAN: A lot more likely than what you say . . .

BAGLEY: About as likely as the tits spread with peanut butter . . .

NOT BALD BUSINESSMAN: D'you mind?

PRIEST: The tits were spread with peanut butter!

BAGLEY: Nonsense.

PRIEST: It says they were. Who's the man you are to think you know more about it than the press?

BAGLEY: I'm an expert on tits. Tits *and* peanut butter.
BAGLEY moves excitedly forward. NOT BALD
BUSINESSMAN *quickly folds his newspaper.*

NOT BALD BUSINESSMAN: Look here. I've had enough of this.

BAGLEY: I'm also an expert drug pusher. I've been pushing drugs for twenty years. And I can tell you, a pusher protects his pitch. Don't like competition see. So we associate a relatively innocuous drug with one that is extremely dangerous. And the rags go along with it because they adore the dough from the ads.

NOT BALD BUSINESSMAN: I've had enough of this. I'm getting off at Datchet.

BAGLEY: Getting off at Datchet won't help you. Getting off anywhere won't help you. I've had an octopus squatting on my brain for a fortnight, and I suddenly see that *I* am the only one who can help you!
The train is slowing down and BAGLEY *is speeding up. And*

all are silenced. And although the expressions are indescribable they are somehow appropriate to the contemplation of a tit and peanut butter expert with an octopus on his head. BAGLEY *rises to his feet.*

It would be pointless to go into the reasons why, but I've been worried sick about boils for a fortnight. Large boils . . . small boils . . . fast erupters . . .

The train jolts to a halt and there's a shared attempt to get out. They're incurable. All of them. I know that, and so does everybody else until they get one. Then the *rules* suddenly change. With a boil on the nose there's a sudden overnight surge in faith.

BALD BUSINESSMAN *gets the door open and is leading the way to the platform.*

They wanna believe something will work.

The PRIEST's *last out. Slams the door.* BAGLEY *tears the window down.*

He knows that, which is why he gets a good look in with the dying. Sells 'em hope you see! But these boys would be full time into real estate if anyone came up with a genuine cure for death.

Several astonished faces are now looking at this maniac preaching from the window. The PRIEST *scuttles up the platform staring back.*

PRIEST: Good God. This is a madman.

The train pulls out and BAGLEY *shouts into the crowd as he passes.*

BAGLEY: What d'you know about God, you wire-haired Mick! Here, have 'em! I've given up!

He throws three packs of cigarettes after the disappearing cleric.

II. INT. KITCHEN. HOUSE. NIGHT.

A lot of money is visible in here. Hi-tech with a fridge the size of a small house. If the kitchen is anything to go by Bagley must own an impressive spread. He sits at a table reading the Guardian. *Behind him a coffee pot climaxes on the hob.* JULIA *bustles in wearing jewels and a chic black dress. Stares at* BAGLEY *in amazement.*

JULIA: What on earth are you doing?

BAGLEY: I'm reading a newspaper.

JULIA: We're in the middle of a dinner party!

She removes the coffee pot and organises half a dozen little cups.

BAGLEY: I'm sorry, I can't bear that great pompous herbivore in there. I'm sick of hearing about her soya proteins.

JULIA: You might at least make a bit of an effort . . . at least sit at the table.

He closes his paper and JULIA *exits instructing him to bring cream.* BAGLEY *finds it in the fridge and follows her into the dining room.*

12. INT. DINING ROOM. HOUSE. NIGHT.

A cello concerto supplies background atmosphere. Firelight and candlelight illuminate silver and impressive antiques. Maybe half a dozen faces around the table. Most will describe themselves as they speak. It's brandy time and the liqueurs are moving about.

PENNY WHEELSTOCK: . . . what utter balls, Jonathan.

This is obviously the pompous herbivore. Thirty-seven years old. No bra and huge tits in a cheesecloth blouse. BAGLEY *sits facing her.*

WHEELSTOCK: Do you think women like filling their bodies with chemicals?

JULIA: We were talking about eels, darling.

Her attempt to involve BAGLEY *results in a vague nod of his head.*

BASIL: Yes, most extraordinary. Apparently by the year 2000 the oestrogen level in the sea will be as much as two parts per million. So many women taking the pill you see. The problem is, it's starting to mess up the fish.

JULIA: They're breeding in the sea.

JONATHAN: I thought fish did.

JULIA: Not *eels*, darling. Eels breed in rivers.

WHEELSTOCK *begins cracking walnuts. A mix of nuts and opprobrium.*

WHEELSTOCK: I think men should bleed.

Eyes disappear into the coffee cups. But BAGLEY *seems to take a sudden interest in the conversation. Sits back in his chair staring hard into the huge expanse of ugliness constituting her face.*

BAGLEY: What a disgusting thing to say.

WHEELSTOCK: You find bleeding disgusting, do you?

BAGLEY: Not particularly. Just the way you said it, with that horrible sneer and mouthful of nuts.

JULIA: Darling. Penny is our guest!

WHEELSTOCK: Women, I might inform you, take that primitive device called the pill because it is all they've got. They don't like it. I personally abhor it. But unfortunately it is all we have got.

BAGLEY: In what context?

WHEELSTOCK: In the context of bed!

BAGLEY: I'm surprised you need to bother.

BASIL: Cointreau anyone?

No takers and the eyes are still in the coffee cups. Only BAGLEY *seems happy with what he's said. He leans back pouring a glass of wine.* JULIA's *eyes seek his and she manufactures an uneasy smile.*

JULIA: Darling, I know you're having a very difficult time at the moment, and I know you've had a lot to drink, and didn't mean what you said. But Penny is our guest, and I'd like you to apologise.

WHEELSTOCK *is scooping a kind of hessian potato bag from the floor.*

WHEELSTOCK: He doesn't need to apologise. Those kind of sexist attitudes are beyond apology.

BAGLEY: What d'you mean by that?

His cynicism is met by a fleshy wall of vitamin-inspired contempt.

WHEELSTOCK: Do you really think I don't understand? You dislike me, because I'm not one of those starved little tarts you exploit. I don't rush out to buy your latest make up. I have a mind of my own, and I have a body of my own, that

136

doesn't fit into the preconceived patterns men like you
dictate.

BAGLEY: You mean you're fat.

PENNY *slams her vegetable sack on the table and bellows at*
BAGLEY.

WHEELSTOCK: *Yes I'm fat.* And you're perfectly at liberty to
hate me for it!

BAGLEY: You're quite wrong. I don't dislike you because of
that. I wouldn't care if you were so huge we had to put up
scaffolding to feed you.

A flurry of activity at the far end of the table as BASIL *stands.*

BASIL: For God's sake, let's not have a row.

BAGLEY: Why not? Why shouldn't we have a row?

JULIA: Because nobody wants one. You're being completely
irrational.

She also stands to witness the pasty frenzy flooding BAGLEY's
dial.

BAGLEY: Irrational? We're all prepared to sit here discussing
mung beans and soya protein, but if anybody touches on
anything real, it's irrational?

JULIA: All right then, you're being rude – unutterably
rude – and a bore.

JONATHAN *is on his way down the table gesturing* BAGLEY
*to a study. He suggests the chaps retire to a safe distance and
share a drink.*

BAGLEY: I've had a drink, thank you. And now I'm having
another.

He swallows his wine in one and again directs himself toward
PENNY.

Do you wear Y-fronts?

BASIL: Don't tell him.

BAGLEY: And if you do, are they *white* clean, *bright* clean, not
a trace of *shite* clean?

WHEELSTOCK: I think you're contemptible.

BAGLEY: And I think you are a vegan who eats meat in
secret – you see! She doesn't deny it. She's a meat-eating
vegan!

Unhappily PENNY *rises to it. Defending her most ardent principles.*

WHEELSTOCK: I do *not* eat meat!

BAGLEY: But you'll eat fish. You'll eat fish till the cows come home.

BASIL: Don't argue with him.

WHEELSTOCK: *Fish* is allowed.

BAGLEY: Including eels? Eels full of oestrogen? If it's buggering the eels, think what it's doing to you.

PENNY makes a bolt for the door. BAGLEY *follows almost dancing in her wake. He shouts delightedly* 'Get back to your fig bottling' *and suddenly everyone is in the hall.* JULIA *at the front door with her friend.* BASIL *and* JONATHAN *cornering* BAGLEY *by a grandfather clock.*

JONATHAN: For God's sake, Bagley. You're going out of control.

BAGLEY: Oh no I'm not! I'm just beginning to see the light!

JONATHAN: You're talking nonsense.

The reply is a bleat of laughter. Both BASIL *and* JONATHAN *move an appropriate distance up the kilim.* PENNY *negotiates the front door.*

BAGLEY: It's all so clear. I've been living a nightmare. Obsessed with other people's acne, racking my brains to be original about boils. I've been going berserk! But then I suddenly thought of a pork pie, and I tell you, it was like a fucking brain wave!

BASIL: Get his Valium.

BAGLEY: Suddenly everything is clear. Not only the priest and his ridiculous tits, but the washing machines as well.

BASIL: What washing machines?

BAGLEY: The top loaders and the gentle-wash options . . .

Sound of a car backfiring and JULIA *re-appears blanching with panic.*

The reverse tumblers and the heavy-soil selectors.

JULIA: Come and try and sit down, darling.

BAGLEY: The rinse holds. The pre-fills and all the other bastards. But not any more. Because I have found out. I have found out – and let no man refute my word – that with every load that gets washed, a brain gets washed with it. I have discovered that brains are being laundered daily. They are being cleansed whiter than any knicker, more thoroughly than any stinking football sock. I have found that out. But it shall be no more.

And like a sinister conclusion the grandfather clock tolls twelve.

13. INT. HALLWAY. HOUSE. DAY.

Bright yellow sunlight and birds singing. JULIA *descends a sweeping staircase under about three-fifths of a hangover. As she passes the grandfather clock it strikes eight. Nothing abnormal about that and she hardly bothers to look. Then she stops and looks hard.*

A string of pork sausages is hooked on the clock and dangling over the dial. A moment of confusion and she rushes towards the kitchen.

14. INT. KITCHEN. HOUSE. DAY.

The view that greets JULIA *roots her to the spot. It will silence her for as long as it takes to describe. It is obvious* BAGLEY *has spent hours emptying cupboards. The kitchen has become a focus of every brand name in the house. The floor is littered with the contents of the deep freeze: random packs of French beans; bricks of melting spinach; ice cream and half a dozen 'Boil Them in the Bag' kippers in various stages of decay. The entire contents of a bathroom cabinet have been emptied into a big saucepan and topped with artificial cream. There's a tureen full of deodorants and electric hair-curlers. Julia's make up has been dumped into a bucket with a good selection from the refrigerator. Bagley has opened every tin and every tube. The result is a colourful mélange of almost indescribable horror. A stomach-capsizing mess of Max Factor and Heinz. And now on to the architect of all this chaos.* BAGLEY *is too busy hacking tea bags to pieces over the sink immediately to notice her arrival. Apart from socks and a shower cap he is stark naked. His head is smeared with shaving cream and there is a rasher of bacon stuck to his ass. Taking a pace towards him* JULIA *catches sight of a bucketful of creamed rice and lipstick. She looks down as a rissole rises between her toes. She gasps faintly and he looks around.*

BAGLEY: Morning, darling. I thought you were having a lie in.

JULIA: A lie in? Jesus Christ, what do you think you are doing?

He smiles understandingly and returns to the taps almost whistling.

BAGLEY: I'm completing a process of natural selection. I'm going through everything in the house and isolating items of genuine worth. All other products, and especially those contaminated with advertising, I am disposing of. That includes all canned and frozen foods, detergents, aerosols, certain electrical goods and your make up.

JULIA *suddenly rushes forward trampling through scattered rissoles.*

JULIA: Have you gone out of your mind?

BAGLEY: I know it's gonna be difficult, darling, but I'll explain properly, and you will understand.

JULIA: For Chrissake! You're covered in tomato sauce. You're going insane!

He adjusts his shower cap and smiles. Pours perfume on his tea bags.

I'm gonna call an ambulance . . .

BAGLEY: I'm sorry, darling, I haven't got time. I've gotta do all the shoe polishes, and then get under the sink. It's gone eight already and I have to be in the office by ten.

JULIA: You can't go. You're under tremendous stress. You can't possibly go to work.

BAGLEY: I'm going in to resign.

He heads across the kitchen, handing her his apple corer on the way.

Now, why don't you trust me and finish these tea bags? You pop them and pour the perfumes on, then you sort of twiddle them down the plug hole.

Bagley (Richard E. Grant) at work.

Bagley and Julia (Rachel Ward) at home.

Her eyes flare towards the sink. She lunges at the perfume bottles.

JULIA: Not the Givenchy! It's irreplaceable.

The still full bottle is salvaged and BAGLEY *foots it for the door.*

Where are you going?

BAGLEY: Upstairs. I'm dismantling the Hoover.

15. INT. STAIRCASE/UPPER HALLWAY. HOUSE. DAY.

BAGLEY *climbs with* JULIA *following, her voice brittle with urgency.*

JULIA: Dennis, listen to me . . . you're under tremendous stress. You were drunk last night and probably don't realise it, but you were totally out of control.

BAGLEY: Maybe I was. But now I've had time to work things out . . . get everything in perspective.

JULIA: Darling, can't you see what you're doing this morning is equally out of control?

BAGLEY: Oh no, you're quite wrong, Julia. There's nothing out of control about me now.

They reach the end of the hallway. He leads the way through a door.

I know exactly what I'm doing now.

16. INT. BATHROOM. HOUSE. DAY.

And what he's done is here in the bathroom. If anything it's in a worse state than the kitchen. Some time in the dead of night he's come in here and behaved like a savage. The bath is full of parts and saturated newspapers. There are newspapers all over the floor.

For some reason he's brought up a pair of frozen chickens and shoved them down the lavatory. A variety of other things have gone in as well. All kinds of electrical components. Wires sprout over the top of the seat with heating elements and condensers dangling from their ends. JULIA *momentarily stares at an entire transistor radio.*

JULIA: God in heaven.

BAGLEY: The sweet stench of revenge.

By now BAGLEY *has clambered into the bath wielding a*

*carving knife. He sits on the edge thrashing around in the mess
of newspaper pulp and wires. The air is so loaded with hair
lacquer* JULIA *finds it difficult to breathe. She stares as he
attacks a vacuum-cleaner nozzle.*

JULIA: Please stop that. I think you're ill.

BAGLEY *is fighting six feet of hose like it's a huge kind of
snake.*

BAGLEY: I'm gonna do those bastard television sets in here.

JULIA: Like you're doing the vacuum cleaner?

BAGLEY: That's right. Except I'm gonna do them better. I'm
gonna turn them on, and do them in the middle of an
advertisement for themselves. I'm going to drown them.

JULIA: You call that 'rational', do you?

BAGLEY: Certainly. Everything I do is rational.

JULIA: Why have you put chickens down the lavatory?

BAGLEY: To thaw them before dismemberment.

*And he grunts with pleasure as the vacuum-cleaner nozzle flies
off.*

JULIA: You're ill, darling. I want you to get out of the bath.

BAGLEY: They feed them on fish. They taste like fish. So I
shall dismember them and return them via the sewers to
the sea.

JULIA: Get out of the bloody bath.

*The frequency of her command freezes him. He turns towards
her and with something of an angelic smile searches for words
to explain.*

BAGLEY: I know this must be all sort of upsetting to you,
darling. But honestly, I assure you of its necessity. It has
to be done, or we'll never be free.

JULIA: From what? What sort of freedom do you think you
can get from hacking a vacuum cleaner to pieces? Look at
you. You've got a polythene bag on your head, you look
stark raving mad! You need rest. You need help. This
cursed pimple cream has got on top of you.

BAGLEY: Which is why I intend to escape.

JULIA: You're not escaping it. You're encouraging it. You're
suffering them yourself.

*His eyes ask the question in a series of blinks. 'What d'you
mean?'*

You're so run down, you've got a boil yourself.

BAGLEY: Me?

JULIA: Yes, a horrid-looking boil sprouting on your neck.
You've never had a boil in your life. You're totally worn
out, both physically, and emotionally.
*He's also out of the bath clearing a small patch in the mirror.
His reflection confirms what she's said. On the right side of his
neck about three inches up from the collar bone is a small but
polished boil.*

BAGLEY: My God. You're right. I've got a boil.

17. INT. RECEPTION. ADVERTISING AGENCY. DAY.
A tiny security TV watches the elevator doors. The
RECEPTIONIST *works the board like her other job's giving
dirty-phone. 'Sullivan Bristol. One moment.' A moment later the
elevator doors open and a sort of peasant walks in. Her eyes raise as*
BAGLEY *approaches the desk. Show scant reaction to his eccentric
garb. He wears a tweed jacket over a track suit. Plus Wellington
boots and a knitted hat.*

BAGLEY: I'm gonna collect something from my office. While
I'm there I want you to get hold of Bristol, and tell him
I'm coming in to see him.

RECEPTIONIST: Mr Bristol's out. (*Into console.*) Sullivan
Bristol?

BAGLEY: I want a call the moment he turns up. And get
me a coupla dispatch boys, I need some equipment
moved.
She nods with disinterest and BAGLEY *hurries up the glass
stairs.*

18. INT. STUDIO/OFFICE. ADVERTISING AGENCY. DAY.
A bright sunny day over the city. BAGLEY *isn't here for the view.
On hands and knees in front of a document chest he sorts through
dozens of posters going back for perhaps as many years. Here are
rubber tyres and breakfast cereals. Brassières and beers. Another*

drawer comes out and he finds what he's looking for. It's the only poster in a clip-glass frame. As he reaches for it he winces with a kind of electric shock. All but barks at the Boil's sudden issue of pain. On the instant MAUD *ushers in a* SHORTASS *wearing overalls.*

SHORTASS: Want something shifted, Governor?

BAGLEY: Yeah, you're gonna need some help. I want that editing desk out, and put in the back of my Range Rover. *He throws him keys and both* MAUD *and the* SHORTASS *disappear. Massaging his macula* BAGLEY *stands and props the poster to look at it.*

It's a black-and-white job divided by a vertical line down the middle. It obviously seeks a documentary effect. On the left side is an old man in a hospital bed with a pair of rubber hoses vanishing into each nostril. His shrivelled head pokes out of a set of striped pyjamas. The tubes make his eyes run and his teeth are out. He is dying of lung cancer. On the right side is a stark black coffin.

Above the bed the words SOFT PACK. *Above the coffin* HARD PACK. *The geography of the ad can probably be most simply described thus:*

Soft Pack	Hard Pack
(bed)	(coffin)

'Dying for a Smoke?'

BAGLEY *might stare for a long time. But the Boil pumps an unexpected throb that sends him reeling to the mirror. He tears at his collar thrusting the feruncle forward for inspection. It seems to have grown a bit. Certainly obtained some colour! The phone buzzes telling him Bristol is back and* BAGLEY *and his poster are on their way.*

19. INT. OFFICE. ADVERTISING AGENCY. DAY.
As BAGLEY *walks in* BRISTOL *senses something other than Wellington boots is afoot. But other than the elevation of the ridge where an eyebrow used to be his reaction to Bagley's appearance is minimal.*

BAGLEY: I've come to give you a present.

BRISTOL: How nice.

BAGLEY removes a poster from the wall and replaces it with his own.

BAGLEY: To me this represents everything that is wrong . . . and everything that is vile with this profession.

BRISTOL: Really?

BAGLEY: It is the reason I'm resigning.

If BRISTOL is surprised he suppresses it. Decides to play this calm.

BRISTOL: What's suddenly upset you about it?

BAGLEY: The hypocrisy it represents.

BRISTOL: It was never used . . .

BAGLEY: Not *its*. Mine. I believed in it, and I sat back like some gagged little idiot while they buggered it. I should have resigned then.

BRISTOL: I see.

BAGLEY: I don't approve of its rejection, I can no longer tolerate it. And I don't approve of Her Majesty's Government's cynical little bit of twaddle that 'Smoking Can Seriously Damage Your Health' as any kind of acceptable alternative.

BRISTOL: I wouldn't have thought anyone was arguing about that.

BAGLEY: Precisely. Nobody's arguing about it. Especially the government. The only fucker this ever frightened was the Chancellor of the Exchequer! But I'm going to argue about it. I'm going to *shout* about it!

BRISTOL: I wouldn't do that, old chap.

BAGLEY: *Can* damage your health? What's *can* gotta do with it? Can! Could! Might! Possibly! Maybe! *Does* is the word we wanna hear, the bastards are killing a hundred thousand a year! '*Warning By Her Majesty's Government*: this product contains highly toxic carcinogenic poisons. Avoid all contact. *Do Not Inhale*. Should inhalation occur seek immediate advice from a physician.'

A faint sheen of perspiration appears on BRISTOL's pate. After contemplating BAGLEY's performance for a second he stands. Moves round to the front of his desk and sits on the edge sucking at his tongue.

BRISTOL: I saw Harry yesterday. He told me you were having one or two problems with the pimple cream.

BAGLEY: Well, he's wrong. Because I have eradicated the pimple cream from my life.

BRISTOL: He also said you'd lost your temper with some photographs.

BAGLEY: That's right. Close ups of hives. Some idiot had snapped a bunch and wanted me to have a look at them.

BRISTOL: But don't you think the way you reacted could be considered a little irrational?

BAGLEY: Don't start the old irrational bollocks with me, Bristol. I'm up to here with it! I know everything there is to know about rationality, and I know everything there is to know about advertising. I've dissected every stinking dream, reduced everything to the lowest common denominator to gratify that unhappy creature the average man. I know every smell his body is capable of producing. I've constructed antidotes for his ugliness, solved intimate problems for his wife's vagina – I've been in his mind, and I know every aspect of his sickening lot. Why? Because I have created it. I've oiled greed and bargained the bad for the disgusting. So don't tell me I'm being irrational because I'm the man who's taken the stench out of everything but shit.

BRISTOL *looks like someone just played a golf ball off the top of his head. His astonishment switches into an expression of concern.*

BRISTOL: Look here, old chap, why don't you take some time off?

BAGLEY: What the fuck do you think I'm resigning for? I'm taking for ever off. I'm going to cleanse my life. I'm going to rid my mind and body of poisons. And when I've done it, I intend to make it my life's work to encourage others to do it.

BRISTOL: And how will you do that?

147

BAGLEY: By telling them, you bald fool.

BRISTOL: Walking up and down with a sandwich board?

BAGLEY: If necessary.

BRISTOL: Advertising, dear boy.

BAGLEY: How dare you! How *dare* you!

The sudden increase in blood pressure does not go unnoticed by the Boil. It pumps out another stab of pain that sends him spinning into the nearest chair. BRISTOL *shunts towards him with apprehension.*

BRISTOL: What's the matter, Bagley?

BAGLEY: I've got a boil. A big boil. I believe it's justice. The poison quitting my miserable system.

While BAGLEY *attempts to appease his lump* BRISTOL *returns to his chair. Settling himself on elbows he affects a fatherly approach.*

BRISTOL: Fifteen years ago, I was out there on the floor where you are now. And I was very like you, Bagley. I was the best. But I'd got myself into some trouble with a gas-fired heating system. I tell you, I was desperate. I made myself ill with worry. I finally ended up at a specialist who told me I'd given myself an ulcer. But it was a lot more than that to me. As far as I was concerned, I'd given myself a 'detonator'. I became obsessed with fears of 'spontaneous combustion'. This gas-fired business had penetrated so deeply into my sub-conscious, I thought I was seconds away from bursting into flames. I started drinking water, sometimes as much as twenty-five pints a day. I slept with a bucketful by the bed. I even bought a fire extinguisher . . .

BAGLEY: I'm surprised you needed to bother. You must have pissed like a fire engine.

BRISTOL *smiles warmly and* BAGLEY *looks across at him with a sneer.*

Anyway, whass all this gotta do with me?

BRISTOL: What I'm telling you is I tried to quit too. But the man who sat here refused to accept my resignation.

BAGLEY: Hard luck.

BRISTOL: Was it? I took a month off and went abroad. Rested and got myself a tan. And then I came back, and by Christ, Bagley, did I sell some radiators . . .

BAGLEY: Really?

BRISTOL: Never been better. And I'll tell you something else, I didn't burst into flames either.

BAGLEY: Well, let's hope it's not too late.

And he stands cupping his bump. His cynicism cancels his warning.

Because if you went up it would save me a job. 'Cause I tell you, Bristol, any night now I'm likely to turn up here and burn this dump to the ground.

He goes out the way he came in and doesn't bother to slam the door.

20. INT. BEDROOM/EN SUITE BATHROOM. HOUSE. NIGHT.

A wedge of light cuts in from an adjoining bathroom. Otherwise the room is in darkness. JULIA is in bed with little hope of sleep. A commentary of clenched expletives is conducted by an unseen Bagley.

BAGLEY (O.S.): I can't believe anything could grow so quickly. This morning it was a pea, now it's like a fucking tomato. I can't bear it any longer, Julia. The bastard's on fire!

This obviously isn't the first time she has been forced out of bed. JULIA arrives in the bathroom (this one mercifully spared from Bagley's rampage). BAGLEY sits on a dining chair in front of a mirror. He wears pyjama trousers and has a naked chest. His back is streaked with a khaki substance. A diluted version of it fills the basin.

JULIA: Bathe it in warm water again.

BAGLEY: I *have* bathed it in warm water again.

The Boil is downwind and unseen. It's also covered with a poultice.

I've washed it, dried it, poked it, agitated it, and insulted it! Nothing. All it does is throb, and get bigger. It's like a *thing* in a medical magazine.

JULIA: Hasn't the mustard helped?

BAGLEY: Of course not.

> *He slumps forward groaning over the basin.* JULIA *takes the mustard pot and studies it as though contemplating some detail in a recipe.*

JULIA: Perhaps we should try the English.

BAGLEY: This is the English.

JULIA: No it's not, darling. It's Dijon with fine herbs.

> *In despair he slides off his chair and ends up draped over the bath.*

> Why don't you take some aspirin?

BAGLEY: *Never.* I'm gonna knife the swine.

> *His suggestion re-animates him.* JULIA *grabs him on the way out. Suddenly they're conducting a sort of haphazard waltz into the bedroom.*

JULIA: Calm down. It's just a big boil. First thing in the morning I'll run you into town and we'll have it looked at. Now come to bed.

> *She climbs back in, while* BAGLEY *drives wild eyes into a hand mirror.*

BAGLEY: Julia . . . it's just grown a hair.

JULIA: It's a quarter to two in the morning. Will you please come to bed.

BAGLEY: Not now.

> *And he throws the little mirror aside and lashes up a dressing gown.*

> I gotta get down there and work.

21. EXT. THE BAGLEY HOUSE. DAY.
This is nice music. Camille Saint-Saëns, Third Symphony in C Minor. And this is a nice house. One of those delightful warm-brick Georgian jobs in about three acres of wooded grounds. Sunlight drenches the roof. Zippa-de-doo-dah! It's a beautiful day! Perfect day for an advert in fact. Up on the chimney are a pair of animated bluebirds (obviously escaped from a Babycham commercial) smiling their beaks off. Cartoon hearts popping in the air above them. They are in love. The lady bluebird is coy and playing a little

hard to get. She takes off, with her lover following. Whizzes arabesques through the lilac and vanishes through an open downstairs window in the lovely house. The boy bird goes after her with Saint-Saëns not far behind.

22. INT. STUDY. HOUSE. DAY.

While the bluebirds flirt around it, there's time for a look at the room. Sherlock Holmes would have felt at home in here. Walls lined with books and paintings. Old button-backed leather couches and antiques. BAGLEY *is sprawled full length on a Chesterfield asleep.*

At the end of the room is a video editing machine. Video cassettes are scattered all over the floor. The TV is still on showing a freeze frame of delicious autumn woods. What could be more appropriate for the lovers? The lady bird disappears into the television screen and evaporates with her boy. Pretty bubbles explode and BAGLEY *wakes up.*

At least he has probably woken up. The room is full of sunshine and the gardens full of twittering birds. Two things are apparent. One: JULIA *isn't here. And two: neither it seems is there any pain in the Boil.*

He rubs at it pleasantly relieved. Heaving himself off the couch he suddenly realises where he is and indeed why he is there. Crossing to the editing machine he flips it off and hurries towards the door.

23. INT. BEDROOM/EN SUITE BATHROOM. HOUSE. DAY.

Almost noon on the bedside clock and the bed already made. Tearing off his dressing gown BAGLEY *motors into the bathroom. His feet are barely through the door before he catches sight of the Boil in the mirror. Again it's downwind and can't be seen. But* BAGLEY *has seen it. Its appearance shorts out everything but his eyes. For approximately five seconds they bulge with an expression of utter disbelief. Saint-Saëns hits it with a mighty blast on the organ! Then his legs give way and he collapses into an enveloping vortex of slow motion.*

As he goes down his hand sweeps a plethora of bottles from a near-by shelf. He hits the tiles like a shot horse. The canisters and bottles bounce around his face. Badedas turning slow-motion cartwheels. Toothpaste and brushes dance a brief ballet in rainbows of coloured liquids. A bar of soap spins away as he drifts into unconsciousness.

24. INT. BATHROOM. HOUSE. DAY.

Some similarities to Psycho *here. Here is a huge close up of an eye on a white tiled floor. The difference is that this one is regaining consciousness. Grasping the lavatory* BAGLEY *pulls himself to his feet. He repositions himself at an angle in front of the mirror. Dare he look at the* BOIL? *Slow as a shadow on a sundial he turns in its direction. A tiny nose appears in profile. Oh God in Heaven it's true!*

It is no longer a Boil. Somehow it's transformed itself into a tiny human head about the size of a small onion. It looks well turned out. Dapper even. Hair neatly parted to one side. It is clean shaven and its expression is friendly. Like him it has bright intelligent eyes.

Its gaze is like a dose of curare. BAGLEY *is paralysed with horror. He steadies himself on the hand basin and opens his mouth in an attempt to scream. His tongue comes out but he can't find any sound. He can hardly breathe. The* BOIL *finally opens its happy little mouth revealing a set of gleaming white teeth. It smiles at* BAGLEY *and winks.*

BOIL: Hiya, handsome.

> *The spell is instantly broken. And he bellows like Attila the Hun.*

25. INT. KITCHEN. HOUSE. DAY.

Meanwhile a middle-aged DAILY *is cleaning up in here. Bagley made a big mess and there's a lot of cleaning to do. While she mops the floor* JULIA *puts the finishing touches to a breakfast tray. Boiled egg and coffee pot. She's just about to add the toast when the kitchen door implodes. The cleaner drops her mop! For an instant* BAGLEY *stands framed in the door. Bright yellow and stark naked. (He must have lost his trousers on the way down.) He looks like he's escaped!*

An instant later he's back on the move. Passes JULIA *at speed and crashes out through the back door.* 'All right, Mrs Wallace, you can go home.' *Only too pleased! And the apron is off before* JULIA *can get to the phone. A hurried conversation takes place. She explains the urgency.* 'Well, will you page him? I need him at once.' *While she speaks she catches glimpses of* BAGLEY *through the kitchen window. He sprints up the herb garden and disappears through a hedge.*

JULIA: All right. Ten minutes. Thank you.

As she replaces the receiver BAGLEY *bursts back into the kitchen.*

BAGLEY: The Boil. The Boil.

Too exhausted to communicate he hangs forward fighting for breath.

It's alive. It lives.

JULIA: What d'you mean?

BAGLEY: It's grown a head. I looked at it in the bathroom mirror and it spoke to me.

She pulls out a chair and gets him into it. He slumps forward over the table. JULIA *takes a good squint at the* BOIL. *He's right about one thing. It's definitely grown bigger. And definitely much angrier. But other than that it's just a normal common or garden boil.*

BAGLEY: Have a look at it.

JULIA: I have, darling.

BAGLEY: What's it doing?

She's at a loss how to play this. Humour him or tell him the truth?

JULIA: Nothing. It's just a large boil.

BAGLEY: Boils don't have ears . . . boils don't have partings in their hair!

JULIA: No, darling. Neither does yours.

She speaks with such conviction that it must be true. Otherwise surely she'd be shocked and running as well. He stares up at her blankly.

I promise you, it's all part of the silly stress you're going through.

The sweat turns to goose pimples. JULIA *smiles and offers her hand.*

Come along. We'll go and look at it together . . .

BAGLEY: I don't think I dare.

JULIA: Shall I tell you what happened? You were dreaming. You dreamt you woke up and went into the bathroom. You may even have sleepwalked in there.

She finds an old picnic blanket in a cupboard and wraps him in it.

You saw your own face in the mirror and it frightened you. Things like that are always happening when people are under dreadful mental stress.

BAGLEY: Do you think so?

JULIA: I'm certain of it.

The door bell rings. She gets him to his feet. Wants him upstairs.

That'll be Doctor Gatty. You'd better go and put something on.

26. INT. STAIRCASE/HALLWAY. HOUSE. DAY.

JULIA *manoeuvres him into the hall. He creeps upstairs as she answers the door. Her manufactured calm collapses as Doctor* GATTY *appears.*

GATTY: What's the problem, Julia?

JULIA: Dennis thinks he's got a talking boil.

GATTY: What?

JULIA: I can't go into it now, but he's manic.

GATTY: Where is he?

JULIA: Upstairs.

GATTY: How's this manifesting?

Here comes the answer. BAGLEY *appears like Dracula at the top of the stairs. His blanket billows out behind him as he comes crashing down at full speed. Both* GATTY *and* JULIA *stand briskly to one side to allow him passage. As soon as he's past* GATTY *gives chase.*

27. EXT. GARDENS. GREENHOUSE. DAY.

BAGLEY *sprints the lengths of the lawns with* GATTY *and* JULIA *in pursuit. Rushing through the marrows* GATTY *manages to head him off and fell him with a rugby tackle outside the greenhouse door. There is a brief but intense struggle amongst some flowerpots.* JULIA *arrives with Gatty's bag and a syringeful of tranquilliser is administered.*

28. INT. BATHROOM/BEDROOM. HOUSE. DAY.

GATTY *is covered in bits of garden. Washes his hands in the basin.*

GATTY: How d'you think he'd react to a suggestion of psychoanalysis, Julia?

Drying his hands he walks back into the bedroom. BAGLEY *is flat on his back deep in chemical sleep. A thermometer juts from his mouth.*

JULIA: Well, he'll agree. He'll have to.

She sits in a distraught state at the end of the bed. GATTY *removes the thermometer. Tries* BAGLEY's *pulse. Everything seems to be OK.*

GATTY: Not necessarily. He's almost certainly convinced of his sanity, in which case it might well be difficult to persuade him a psychiatrist could help. I should think the only thing he'd consent to at the moment is me lancing his boil.

JULIA: Why don't you? Do it now while he's asleep?

GATTY shakes his head squashing JULIA's *little burst of enthusiasm.*

GATTY: I'm not an expert in these things, Julia, but I don't think that's a good idea. Removing it in his condition might set up some kind of permanent block. Do you think I could have another small whisky?

29. INT. STAIRCASE/DRAWING ROOM. HOUSE. DAY.

GATTY *and* JULIA *descend the stairs into the gloss of a polished hall.*

GATTY: You've got to remember as far as he's concerned I wouldn't be lancing it I'd be decapitating it. And that

155

could be dangerous. We don't know who this person is. It might be a relative. His mother.

JULIA: It's a male.

GATTY: Father then.

They arrive in the hall and JULIA *leads the way into a drawing room.*

No, I'm sure that before any attempt is made to get rid of it, we've got to find out who it is. And when we've done that, we've got a good chance of converting it back into a normal boil.

She hands him a big slug of Scotch. Returns to pour one for herself.

Then I'll lance it. But at the moment, it's just a matter of getting him in to see a good psychoanalyst.

JULIA: Do you know someone?

GATTY: I know a very good man in town, but it might take two or three days.

JULIA: Then he'll have to consent. And if he doesn't, we'll have to make him.

GATTY: I fear so.

JULIA: What d'you mean?

GATTY: It would involve certification.

JULIA: But he's just exhausted. He's not really – mad, is he?

GATTY: Running naked round a garden insisting a boil has spoken to you, is more than just exhaustion, Julia.

There is a silence while JULIA *absorbs the nightmarish implications.*

Look, this is what I suggest. Tomorrow I'll call you with an appointment, and you'll have to do your best to get him there. For the moment, make sure he takes the tablets every two hours and he'll stay under control. When he wakes up try and be normal. Cook him dinner.

The drink is finished and they are on their way to the front door.

You'll probably have to go along with him a bit. It'll be difficult, but you'll have to try. And you'd better keep a record of what the boil says, at least, what he says it says.

156

It might be important. Don't worry, we'll sort it out.

And a minute later JULIA *watches his car vanishing down the drive.*

30. INT. KITCHEN. HOUSE. DUSK.

The evening is heavy. Thunder is rolling somewhere in the distance. JULIA *is busying herself in front of the Aga. She turns to toss a salad and* BAGLEY *walks in. He looks like some minor character from a Tolstoy novel. Stubbled and still groggy from the tranquillisers. A bandage circles his neck. His face is the colour of a canned pear. She looks up with a smile. Positions him in a chair and pours a cup of tea. Only the thunder and he watches in silence. Neither exchange anything but eyes until she produces a small vial of blue pills.*

BAGLEY: What are those?

JULIA: Just pills. Two now. Two before bed.

She shakes a pair out and pops them in his mouth. He swallows them without protest. With oozing eyes he watches her work at the cooker. A large casserole comes out filling the atmosphere with steam.

BAGLEY: Do you think I'm going mad, Julia?

JULIA: Goodness gracious, no. Doctor Gatty says you're simply paying the price for your creativity. You have such an active imagination it's taking advantage of you.

BAGLEY: What did he say about the Boil?

JULIA: He said it's perfectly normal. He said it's an absolutely normal boil, and that as soon as you've had a proper rest, it'll go away.

BAGLEY: Are you sure?

JULIA: Absolutely. Trust me and take my word for it.

She consoles him with a tiny smile. Takes the lid off the casserole.

BOIL: Mmmm – smells good – smells thumb-suckin' good.

JULIA: Thank you, darling.

BAGLEY: I didn't say anything.

Another sweet smile from JULIA *as she attempts to go along with him.*

157

JULIA: Oh, I see. Now, we'll have a nice dinner, and everything will be normal.

Nobody could ignore the anxiety in his face but JULIA *does her best.*

And if it speaks again, we'll ignore it? Won't we? Promise?

A long pause and BAGLEY *agrees and she kisses the side of his head.*

Now, you've got ten minutes before I serve, so why don't you go and have a quick bath?

She turns away to deal with saucepans and BAGLEY *hunches a shoulder.*

BOIL: Take the stress out of the day. Relax your aching body. Spoil and pamper yourself in a sea of soothing blue bubbles.

JULIA: Exactly, darling. Off you go then.

Sweat breaks out on BAGLEY's *forehead and he starts tapping fingers.*

BAGLEY: I don't think I really want a bath. I think I'll stay here and watch you cook.

Another groan of thunder and she smiles understandingly. As she returns her casserole to the cooker there is a spasm in BAGLEY's *neck. He ignores it and a sort of sheepish grin spreads over his face as he concentrates on being normal. He stands up. Whistles once. Sits down again.* JULIA *turns and he looks at her with his abnormal smile.*

JULIA: What are you doing?

BAGLEY: Merely whistling.

He whistles again and grips the edge of the table as though it is the edge of his sanity. His mind races for something normal to say.

JULIA: You're staring.

BAGLEY: Not at all. I was just getting ready to clear my throat, that's all.

And he clears his throat and continues staring and tapping as she strains the peas. And BAGLEY *sees something he can be normal about.*

It's extraordinary how much steam comes off hot peas, isn't it?

JULIA: Yes, darling.

BOIL: Go to France.

BAGLEY: Yes. Fancy France? Paris in the springtime?

JULIA: That would be lovely.

He puckers his lips to whistle a little bit of 'Paris in Springtime'.

BAGLEY: That's a very attractive oven glove.

He adjusts the collar of his dressing gown as she butters the peas.

BOIL: Are you ashamed of your false teeth?

JULIA: I don't have false teeth.

BAGLEY: I know you don't, darling. I know you don't. What I meant was, if you *did* have false teeth, would you be ashamed of them? It was a hypothetical question.

JULIA: Probably not.

While she dusts the potatoes with parsley BAGLEY *continues to tap and blink and clear his throat.* JULIA *shuttles to the cooker. Sits at the other end of the table and removes the lid of her casserole.*

JULIA: Boeuf Bourguignon.

Expressing approval BAGLEY *lowers his nose into the cloud of steam.*

BOIL: Breath. For many the unmentionable.

A small discharge of considerable panic escapes along BAGLEY's *lip.*

JULIA: I beg your pardon, darling?

BAGLEY: Just happened to be thinking about it. Breath, and false teeth, and things . . .

Without visible reaction JULIA *takes his plate and ladles out the* boeuf. BAGLEY *offers her potatoes. Gets his chance for small talk.*

BAGLEY: You know, there's no real reason why we should wait . . .

JULIA: For what?

BAGLEY: Paris. We could leave in a week or so? We could even leave tomorrow?

JULIA: You've dropped your napkin.

BAGLEY: I'll buy a couple of polo necks, and we could hop on a plane.

She evades the suggestion by reminding him of his napkin again. He bends down to retrieve it and momentarily vanishes under the table.

BOIL: Put an end to the miseries of dentures. You could smile again with confidence. Just ask Barbara Simmonds.

When his head reappears she lowers her fork with notable precision.

JULIA: Why did you say that? (*No answer.*) Who is Barbara Simmonds?

BAGLEY: I don't know.

JULIA: Then why talk about her?

BAGLEY: I don't know.

Something welling up in JULIA. *She takes it out on a single potato.*

JULIA: You're not really trying, you know.

BAGLEY: Trying what?

JULIA: Trying not to talk about breath, and false teeth and people with names like 'Barbara Simmonds'.

BAGLEY *shakes his head and lowers his voice in a clenched whisper.*

BAGLEY: I *am*, Julia. It's got nothing to do with me. It's the you know what.

JULIA: Well it's ever so slightly getting on my nerves.

BAGLEY: I thought we weren't going to listen to it.

JULIA: I can't help but listen to it.

BAGLEY: And I can't stop the you know what saying it.

JULIA: Stop saying the you know what.

BAGLEY: All right then, the Boil.

JULIA: Darling, it's not the Boil. Don't you think I haven't noticed? Everytime you say something you turn away, hunch a shoulder, or get under the table so I can't see your lips moving.

BAGLEY: That's not the case, Julia. I'm not turning away to

speak. What it's doing is waiting till I turn away before *it* speaks.

JULIA: That's nonsense. It was you that suggested France.

BAGLEY: I did not. I merely confirmed what the Boil said.

JULIA: Then stop siding with it!

BAGLEY: Don't be ridiculous, I'm not siding with it. I'm going crazy trying to incorporate it into my conversation so I won't upset you. But I never know what it's going to say next.

JULIA: What *you'll* say next. It's *you* saying it.

BAGLEY: The Boil, Julia. Believe me, it's the *Boil*.

JULIA: Well, I can't stand it any more.

BAGLEY: How d'you think I feel about it? I'm on the coast of panic, I'm staring over the edge.

JULIA: Just tell me how a boil could come up with a name like Barbara Simmonds?

Saliva floods BAGLEY's *mouth as he struggles for remnants of sanity.*

BAGLEY: Say no more, Julia. Don't say more.

JULIA: Why should a boil suddenly suggest going to France?

BAGLEY: I don't know.

JULIA: Why not Portugal?

BAGLEY: I don't know. I don't know. Perhaps the fucker wants to go up the Eiffel Tower. Maybe the bastard wants to see the sights!

A crease of lightning outside. JULIA *stands and so does her husband.*

JULIA: *Sit down.* I'm gonna call Gatty.

BAGLEY: What for?

JULIA: To see if he's got you in.

BAGLEY: In where?

Wide eyed, he moves fast round the table towards his retreating wife.

JULIA: Stay back! You need help!

BAGLEY: I refuse to have that quack in here. I refuse to be rendered unconscious!

JULIA: You've got to see a psychiatrist.

A thunder clap shakes the foundations. BAGLEY *heads for the gardens.*

31. INT. STUDY. HOUSE. DAY.
The curtains are drawn and the room in darkness. Considerable degeneration is evident. Old magazines and leaflets strewn everywhere. Empty cups and half-eaten sandwiches under a rubble of video cassettes. The door is barricaded with a chair under the knob. Another chair in the middle of the room on which sits BAGLEY. *Grimy bandages cover his* BOIL. *About three days' beard. Plus a cardboard box on his head (probably a wine case or something similar). The front has been cut off and a hole cut into the bottom to accommodate his neck.*

BAGLEY: Are you there, Julia? Are you there?

He peers out like a loony whispering through bars. There's a haunted look in his eyes. And he looks like a nitwit playing television.

I have to be very quiet. He's a very light sleeper. I wish I could come out and talk to you, darling . . . But it's impossible. You've seen. I have to tell you, Julia, I'm getting increasingly concerned for my future.

At first appearance he's talking to himself. But a change of angle reveals a tripod with a little Sony video camera clamped to its top.

I don't know how this'll end. For all I know in a fortnight's time I'll be waking up with a bald head and a bit of a grin. 'How d'you feel Mr Bagley?' 'Much better thank you, Doctor.' But one thing I'm not, darling, is insane. I'm one hundred per cent sane. When I came in here it was my intention to make a film. I wanted to tell the world about advertising. Haven't finished it of course. It's difficult to concentrate with a chancre yakking on your neck. (Incidentally, in case it's bothering you, the reason I'm wearing this wine carton on my head is so I can talk without disturbing it. It can't hear me, you see.)

But just in case it might he leans a little closer into the camera.

The world is in danger, Julia. The greed is out of

control – greed is abolishing the future. It's turning truth inside out and upside down. And *this* is its poisonous 'mouthpiece'.

A buffalo farts under the bandages. BAGLEY's *face laces with panic.*

Oh, Christ, I've woken him up – I'll have to be quick – what I have to explain is the mechanics of a holocaust.

He lowers his voice a point or two and the BOIL *whispers* 'Oh dear.'

And I'm not talking about atom bombs, darling. I'm talking about hamburgers.

BOIL: Oh dear, Oh dear.

BAGLEY: I know that must sound pretty controversial coming from a man with a speaking chancre and a cardboard box on his head, but I'll explain.

BOIL: I could do with an hamburger.

For reasons best known to itself the BOIL *adopts the voice of a ruffian.*

BAGLEY: Don't listen! Just listen to me!

BOIL: I could actually murder for a fuckin' hamburger.

BAGLEY: There are millions and millions of hamburgers, Julia.

BOIL: Swing for it!

BAGLEY: And if something isn't done to stop them, they'll end up destroying us all.

BOIL: How about cheeseburgers?

BAGLEY: Hamburgers are coming out of the rain forests in their millions.

BOIL: Deal with cheeseburgers?

BAGLEY: Hamburgers are coming from Brazil.

BOIL: How about cheeseburgers?

BAGLEY: Yes! Cheeseburgers too!

BOIL: Pork pies?

BAGLEY: Pork pies have nothing to do with it!

BAGLEY almost knocks his box off. Attempts to control his emotions.

BOIL: I had a nasty feeling I was gonna have to wake up to
   this. (*Sniffs.*) If I was you, I'd turn this off Julia. It's only
   gonna upset ya.
BAGLEY: You see what a nightmare I'm in? You see why I
   can't talk to you?
BOIL: Who are you talking to, then?
BAGLEY: God it *converses*. I'm talking to *it*.
BOIL: I need a cigarette.
BAGLEY: Be silent, you Moloch.
BOIL: Moloch?
BAGLEY: Yes, yes, you, you Moloch. You bogy.
BOIL: If you insist we have to listen to this bullshit, I need a
   cigarette.
   BAGLEY's *desperation is terminal. And he grabs at a floating
   straw.*
BAGLEY: All right, I'll get you one. On *one condition* – that
   you keep quiet while you're smoking it.
BOIL: Deal.
BAGLEY: Swear?
BOIL: I might be a 'chancre', but my word is my bond.
BAGLEY: Don't turn off, darling. Sixty seconds, and I'll be
   back.

32. INT. KITCHEN. HOUSE. DAY.
BAGLEY *moves like a burglar in his own house. Obviously anxious
in case someone grabs him. Not having much success finding
cigarettes. He checks several drawers and cupboards before spotting
an old bag by the door. He starts searching it when* MRS
WALLACE *appears. Both are startled by the other. Clear from her
expression that it's her bag. And also clear that she doesn't fancy
being alone with* BAGLEY.
BAGLEY: Oh, Mrs Wallace! I didn't know you were here.
   Thought everyone was out.
WALLACE: My husband's outside in the van.
BAGLEY: Is he?
   BAGLEY *stares from his box and her fist tightens on the mop
   handle.*

164

How is he?

WALLACE: He's waiting to collect me.

BAGLEY: Is he? Julia out shopping? Look, I wasn't actually going through your handbag. I need a cigarette.

A pack is produced instantly from her apron and she hands it across.

WALLACE: Here. You can have them all.

BAGLEY: I only want one. I don't smoke.

He shoves a cigarette in and cranes towards her with a slight grin.

Got a light?

A match comes at arm's length. A single inhalation buckles his face.

Vile. I'm glad I've given up.

He's poised to exit when JULIA *suddenly arrives with grocery sacks.*

Morning, darling. Lovely day.

JULIA: Is it? The traffic's appalling.

Paying no attention to BAGLEY's *box she dumps her bags on the table.*

Wouldn't make me a cup of tea, would you, Silvia? Tea, Dennis?

BAGLEY: No thank you.

Still paying no attention to his box she starts to unload groceries.

Don't pretend you haven't noticed my cardboard box, Julia, because I know you have. And I know Mrs Wallace, God bless her, has noticed it too. But there's a perfectly reasonable explanation which I'm afraid I don't have time to get into now.

JULIA *hits him with a sweet smile. It translates as 'I see, darling.'*

Matter of fact, I'm very busy now. I'd better get back in there. Thank you for the cigarette, Mrs Wallace.

JULIA: I thought you'd given up, Dennis.

BAGLEY: I have. I'm not smoking it. I'm just holding it. I'll be out later.

JULIA *manages a final instruction before he vanishes into the hall.*

JULIA: Well don't be too long. We're leaving in less than an hour.

33. INT. PSYCHIATRIST'S SURGERY. CITY. DAY.

Everything about this place is calm. The colours are white and pale green. But indisputably the calmest thing in the room is the man who works here. DOCTOR SOLOMON MENDLEBAUM *is fifty-two years old with an American stain in his voice and a well-stocked tan. He's also quite obviously rich. Looking around in here it's apparent there are a lot more well-shod maniacs about than most of us would care to imagine.*

BAGLEY *sits at the trade side of his desk in jeans and a sweater. A yard of bandages is wrapped around his neck. He waits in silence as* MENDLEBAUM *makes a lengthy perusal of Gatty's covering letter. After a suitable period the* DOCTOR *removes his gold rims and smiles across.*

MENDLEBAUM: Who's going to tell me about it, then? You, or the Boil?

BAGLEY *can't believe his ears. The tactic puts him on the defensive.*

BAGLEY: No, no, I think we should start again. There's no *side* to any of this. There is me. There is a Boil. The Boil happens to be able to speak, but that doesn't qualify it to give an opinion. It was me who decided to come here, not it.

MENDLEBAUM: You don't think the inclusion of the Boil could perhaps help us?

BAGLEY: No, I'm not interested in its opinions.

MENDLEBAUM: Even if it says something that might be of relevance?

BAGLEY: I'm not interested in it no matter what it says. In my opinion it should be lanced instantly. That's the only reason I agreed to come off the garage roof. If it wants to join in it can pay its own bill.

For the moment MENDLEBAUM *decides to agree. He stands*

166

and gestures BAGLEY *to a pale-green leather couch.*
Scepticism shrugs BAGLEY'*s shoulders but he reluctantly*
assumes the full-length traditional position. Once he's settled
MENDLEBAUM *begins a slow stroll around his office.*

MENDLEBAUM: Tell me about advertising.

The remark sounds ridiculous. BAGLEY *rolls eyes under closed lids.*

You resigned from an important firm with a very highly paid job. I'd like to know your reasons – at least, try and give me an example of even one of those reasons.

BAGLEY: All right. Reason one. Advertising conspires with Big Brother.

MENDLEBAUM: And you are afraid of Big Brother? Someone, or something, coming into your life and telling you what to do?

BAGLEY: No, I'm not afraid of him. I'm one of the few who really understands him.

MENDLEBAUM: Oh?

BAGLEY: The man who conceived of Big Brother never knew what was coming down the line. Thought his filthy creation was gonna be watching us. But it is *us* who watch *it*. There's one in every living room. And the monstrous injustice of it is we peer at it of our own free will.

MENDLEBAUM: You see television as a dictator?

BAGLEY: Of course, and a corrupted one. Every stinking transistor has been contaminated with greed and waste and despair. It's putrid with advertising and propaganda. And advertising is a liar. It's a monster that won't be satisfied until it's destroyed this entire planet.

MENDLEBAUM: So we can say, principally, that it is television that you blame?

BAGLEY: We can say *entirely* it is the crooks who have infiltrated it that I blame. They've moved in on the greatest means of communication since the wheel! And now they've done it, their greed is insatiable. They're cutting down jungles to breed hamburgers. Turning the whole world into a car park. They'd sell off the sea to

167

satisfy the needs of their great god Greed. And it won't be satisfied till we're all squatting in one of its fucking hatchbacks on a motorway. But there isn't gonna be anywhere left to go. Except in slow revolutions towards the crest of the next slag heap.

MENDLEBAUM: Do you have trouble in getting an erection?

BAGLEY: What?

MENDLEBAUM: Can you get an erection?

BAGLEY: Yes.

MENDLEBAUM: Masturbating much?

BAGLEY: *Constantly.* I've got a talking Boil on my neck! What would you do?

MENDLEBAUM *allows the exchange to settle before reading from a pad.*

MENDLEBAUM: What does this mean to you? 'Are you ashamed of your false teeth? Put an end to the miseries of dentures. You could smile again with confidence. Just ask Barbara Simmonds.'

BAGLEY: The Boil said it a few nights ago. It sounds like a particularly crude voice over.

MENDLEBAUM: Voice over?

BAGLEY: The voice that sells. If you're selling perfume it sounds like a lover. If you're selling something inedible you want people to eat, it'll sound as stupid as they'll have to be to buy it. In this case it would sound like a dentist. Someone in the know.

MENDLEBAUM: I see. One could say it is the voice of authority? Like a parent's voice, almost?

BAGLEY: If you like.

MENDLEBAUM: Has the Boil spoken this morning?

BAGLEY: Yes, I had a row with it. And it got very heated when I refused to shave.

MENDLEBAUM: Tell me about your parents?

BAGLEY: Not part of the plot. As far as I know they were completely normal. I come from a completely normal family.

BOIL: Tell him about your grandfather.

BAGLEY: That was the Boil! Ignore it!

MENDLEBAUM: I don't think we should do that. It's the first time it's spoken in front of me, and it might be important.

BAGLEY: It has nothing important to say. It is destructive, self-satisfied, and abusive.

BOIL: You cunt.

BAGLEY: You see. Don't listen to it.

BOIL: Come on, fair's fair. You've had your say, now I'll have mine.

BAGLEY: Don't listen to it. Don't listen to it.

MENDLEBAUM: Why don't you tell me about your grandfather? If you tell me, the Boil may be quiet.

BAGLEY's *head is suddenly full of confusion. Taking a deep breath he ploughs fingers through his hair and grinds fingertips into his eyes.*

BAGLEY: My grandfather was caught molesting a wallaby in a private zoo in 1919.

MENDLEBAUM: A wallaby?

BAGLEY: It may have been a kangaroo. I'm not sure.

MENDLEBAUM: Sexually?

BAGLEY: I suppose so. He had his hand in its pouch.

BOIL: Fucked it, didn't he?

BAGLEY: *He did not fuck it.*

MENDLEBAUM: Just lie back. What happened to him?

BAGLEY: He pleaded insanity and got three months.

MENDLEBAUM: Does the authoritarian attitude they took with him upset you?

BAGLEY: No, he died before I was born.

MENDLEBAUM: Do you sympathise with him?

BAGLEY: If I'd been stuck in a trench for three years I might do something stupid myself.

MENDLEBAUM: Like showing affection for an animal?

BOIL: He'd fuck one.

BAGLEY: Shut up!

BOIL: Ask Barbara Simmonds. He's fucked her as well.

BAGLEY *leaps from the couch and pirouettes across the surgery. For a moment it seems he's after the paperweight to*

169

bash his affliction. But as he arrives at the desk all colour drains from his face, and he collapses into the nearest armchair like a stringless puppet.

BAGLEY: Oh my God. How could the Boil have known about my grandfather? That means it can read my mind.
It is clear from MENDLEBAUM's *expression that he finds nothing extraordinary in* BAGLEY's *revelation. He calmly reseats himself behind his desk.*

MENDLEBAUM: No, Mr Bagley, it does not. But we shall speak about that in a moment, when we've had a look at this Boil.

BAGLEY: What you mean is you want *me* to have a look at it.
Precisely what MENDLEBAUM *wants. The concept chills* BAGLEY's *marrow.*
No.

MENDLEBAUM: What would you say if I said you don't want to look at it because you are frightened of what you might see?

BAGLEY: I'd say you'd be absolutely right.

MENDLEBAUM: But isn't that trying to pretend it doesn't exist? And isn't that what you're accusing everyone else of doing? We have to reduce this guilt in two ways. First, it must be physically reduced with surgery. And second, we must reduce your punishing conscience by refusing to allow it to hide.
MENDLEBAUM *means business and is heading towards* BAGLEY's *bandages.*
Once we've got it out into the open it'll be easier to fight. And I'm certain, that by the time your neck has healed you will be smiling at this problem and be back at work.

BAGLEY: Never. No matter what you reduce I will never go back to advertising.

MENDLEBAUM: Perhaps. But now let's have a look at this bully on your neck.
Midway through the unwinding MENDLEBAUM *loses his enthusiasm. An unpleasant-looking stain appears through the gauze.* BAGLEY *is left to deal with the last couple of feet on*

170

his own. When the BOIL *is free even the Doctor is shocked by
its proportions. It's assumed all the morbid proportions of a
carbuncle. It is taut and shining and bright green with
antiseptic. With straw around it it could sell as a melon.*

A large gilt mirror hangs over the fireplace.

MENDLEBAUM *coaxes* BAGLEY *towards it. His reflection
finally appears next to the Doctor's. Wan as a shallot his
whole face looks like it's been left in to soak.*

MENDLEBAUM: Just look at it in the mirror. Tell me what you
see.

BAGLEY *manages to get his head up. His pupils dilate
uncontrollably.*

BAGLEY: God in heaven. It's grown a moustache!

For a moment BAGLEY *manages to stand his ground. The*
BOIL *is flushed and puffing. This is understandably due to its
sudden liberation from the bandages. But the reason for the
full-sized Edwardian moustache is less apparent. As it
straightens out like a dragonfly's wings he gasps at the span of
it. The* BOIL *shows little interest in* BAGLEY *or his
psychiatrist. Its attention is directed exclusively into the mirror
with evident concern for its toilet. After a manipulation of lips
it spits hard on the floor and its eyes contact* BAGLEY's *with
aggression.*

BAGLEY: Oh . . . my God.

MENDLEBAUM: Yes. Yes.

The world is about to fall down. And BAGLEY *is about to fall
with it.*

BAGLEY: The bastard looks just like me.

*And a second later the Doctor has an unconscious patient at his
feet.*

34. INT. LONG CORRIDOR. HOSPITAL. NIGHT.

A series of dismal neon lights illuminate BAGLEY's *face as he
passes under them. He is full length on a hospital trolley. About 95
per cent unconscious. Just the sound of the* ORDERLY's *feet
squeaking on the polished floors. Plus a voice echoing somewhere a
long way away.*

MENDLEBAUM (*V.O.*): What you must understand is it is not the Boil that can read you. It is you, Mr Bagley, that can read the Boil. You can read it because it *is* you, at least, a part of you. The Boil knows what you are thinking because you have projected some of you into it. You have given it the side that you find intolerable. The bullying, aggressive, dictatorial side. The side that sells toothpaste and soup.

35. INT. PRIVATE ROOM. HOSPITAL. NIGHT.

The room is in virtual darkness. BAGLEY *is on his back in grey shadows. Brain warming like an ancient TV. The camera is above his bed. It moves slowly in at about the speed of his returning consciousness.*

MENDLEBAUM (*V.O.*): You have decided that selling these things is a bad thing for you to do and you are unable to accept the guilt for what you feel you have done. Therefore, you have transmitted these qualities into the Boil. Perhaps by doing this you hoped to escape your guilt. But you have created a symbol of foul-mouthed authority instead. Your very own Big Brother.

BAGLEY's *eyes snap open into close up of his heavily stubbled face. He slowly assembles his surroundings. A phone on a table by the bed. He tries to reach for it but fails. A smiling little* NURSE *walks in.*

NURSE: Welcome back. My name's Deborah.

BAGLEY: Have they done it?

The large bandaged lump on his neck is sufficient reply. But she answers anyway. At the same time she shoves a thermometer into his face.

NURSE: In the morning. Are you hungry?

BAGLEY: No.

NURSE: I'll bring you something anyway. There's beefburgers, or fish fingers . . .

Out comes the thermometer giving him a chance to express his anxiety.

BAGLEY: I can't move my arms. Can't move anything.

Bagley with the psychiatrist (John Shrapnel).

Julia speaks to the Boil.

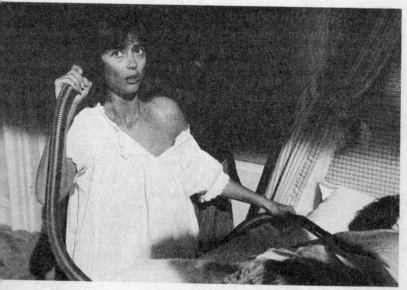

NURSE: Barbiturates. They gave you a whopping dose.

And before BAGLEY *can pursue it she has evaporated through the door. The light goes on as she leaves. He stares up at it trying to get into focus. A mildly remonstrative voice escapes through the bandages.*

BOIL: You should have had the fish fingers.

BAGLEY's eyes close in loathing. The BOIL *adopts a pirate's voice.*

Mouth-waterin' fillets of young cod, matey. In crisp golden batter my mate!

BAGLEY: *Shut up.* You never talk in front of people, so don't talk in front of me.

The BOIL *sniffs under its wrappings. It'll now revert back to cockney.*

BOIL: Suit yourself. Suit yourself. Suit yourself. Just thought you might be interested in a little light rabbit to while the time away. Fuck me, what I wouldn't do for a cigarette.

The BOIL *whistles a little sea shanty between its teeth.*

BAGLEY attempts to roll his head to smother it but everything refuses to move.

BAGLEY: Who are you? What do you want?

BOIL (*in French accent*): Aye yam your better 'alfff . . .

BAGLEY: You are not.

BOIL (*French accent*): *Mais oui, je suis.* A very exponseev pseechiatrist told *yuuu* aye wazzz.

BAGLEY: He did not! You're just a dirty carbuncle!

BOIL (*cockney again*): There's no reason to raise your voice. There's no reason why we shouldn't pass these last few hours together amicably.

BAGLEY: Be quiet.

BOIL: That wouldn't be fair. I listened to you and all that Big Brother muck. I don't mind telling you I was bored stiff. Had absolutely nothing to do under there – 'cept tend me tash of course. Here, do you know why I grew it? Big 'Granddad'.

BAGLEY: How did you find out about my grandfather?

BOIL: Walls have ears, Dennis. I overheard Julia telling Gatty.

174

(Nice paira tits, Julia.) I believe you were unconscious at
the time.

BAGLEY: You bastard. I only wish one thing. And that is that I
could be awake to see you lanced. I'd like to see the knife
going in. I'd like to see you suffer!

BOIL: A typically Communist statement.

BAGLEY: I'm not a Communist.

BOIL: Yes you are. You wanna take everyone's car away.

BAGLEY: I do not wanna take anything from anyone. I want to
give them the choice of something better.

BOIL: Oh yes, what?

BAGLEY: Trains.

BOIL: *Trains?* Trains are no good. They're old-fashioned. I
hate trains. They're rotten.

BAGLEY: Only because they don't consume. Only because
they're already there, and don't eat up more and more and
more. That's why you hate them. That's why
'government' hates them. That's why they're
old-fashioned and rotten.

BOIL: You Commies don't half talk a lot of shit.

BAGLEY: Shut up. I'm not a Communist, and I refuse to argue
with a carbuncle.

BOIL: You are a Communist.

BAGLEY: Fuck off!

NURSE: That's very rude of you, Mr Bagley. Nobody's forcing
you to have supper.

BAGLEY: I'm sorry, it wasn't directed at you.

*Like most in her profession she is quick to accept apology and
is smiling again as she manoeuvres a trolley over the bed. A
steel lid is lifted revealing four lozenges of tangerine-coloured
fish and a compliment of bright green peas. Hard to imagine
anything more vile.*

BOIL: Lovely.

NURSE: Thought you'd change your mind.

BAGLEY: That wasn't me. That was the Boil.

NURSE: I've heard all about your Boil, Mr Bagley. Now you
tuck in and enjoy it.

175

BAGLEY: It's no good. Even if I wanted it I couldn't eat. I can't move my arms.

NURSE: Looks like you're doing fine to me.

And indeed his right arm is busily shaking a bottle of tomato sauce. BAGLEY *is speechless with horror. Tries to detain the exiting* NURSE.

BAGLEY: Oh my God. Nurse. Nurse. It's the Boil shaking it. It's the Boil.

But it's too late because she's gone. BAGLEY *is suddenly drenched in sweat. Concurrently there is a terrible sound. Like a hawser straining to hold a barge. The* BOIL *is expanding rapidly. Its muscular inflation stretches the bandages to breaking point. A tuft of hair is visible. Like a black and white pineapple.* BAGLEY *is manic with fear. Because now the* BOIL *is very purposefully beginning to unwind bandages and at the same time beginning to rewind them over* BAGLEY's *face.*

BAGLEY: Jesus, help me. Nurse. Nurse.

BOIL: You think I'd let a little pipsqueak like you undermine society? Ruin everything we've got? Piss like you needs dealing with! You're the enemy within!

BAGLEY *continues squealing for the nurse. The* BOIL *tries to silence him with sheets. It manages partially to obscure* BAGLEY's *head and swing its own into an upright position. Here it completes the removal of the bandages. They unwind down the face. The face is an identical full-sized replica of Bagley's! Its mouth buckles into a smile.*

BAGLEY (*O.S.*): Nurse. Nurse. Nurse.

As she re-appears the BOIL *again attempts to drown* BAGLEY *with sheets.*

BOIL: D'you think I could have a pillow?

They exchange smiles and she obliges with a pillow behind its head.

BOIL: Thank you, Debbie. May I call you Debbie?

Not only has it copied BAGLEY's *face. It has also copied his speech.*

BAGLEY (*O.S.*): You're talking to the *wrong* head.

176

BOIL: Sorry, dear, I get these nasty spasms.

BAGLEY (*O.S.*): Help. Help. Help.

DEBORAH has already left to get it. The BOIL bellows at his BAGLEY.

BOIL: Shut up. I've had enough of you.

The BOIL is now in total control of BAGLEY's muscles. Fingers close round the fish fingers and stoke them into the BOIL's mouth. The other hand deals with the ketchup bottle smearing each fish finger as it goes in. When the meal is finished the bottle is upended and the BOIL quaffs what is left of it in one. The gobbling is furious with much smacking of lips. As the empty bottle crashes to the floor two pairs of rubber soles come squelching at a fast pace to the bedside.

BAGLEY (*O.S.*): Help. Help. Help.

A well-spoken Pakistani takes one look at the voice-throwing mouthful of ketchup and prescribes an immediate dose of unconsciousness.

No, No. It's the *Boil*. The *Boil*.

HOSPITAL DOCTOR: Don't worry, old man. You have a little sleep. It'll all be over in the morning.

The bedclothes are drawn aside. BAGLEY is still raving under sheets. A pair of hands are clamped to an arm. Maybe he feels the needle go in, but certainly little else. There is an instant voltage reduction.

BAGLEY (*O.S.*): *Wrong head*. You're gonna lance the *wrong*

A fuse out as the barbiturates hit. Everything else is mere static.

head.

36. EXT. COUNTRY ROAD. DAY.

Widor's Fifth Symphony blasts at maximum amps. This could be an ad but it isn't. It is reminiscent of a commercial for British Airways, starring Concorde. On a very long lens. Heat haze shimmers on the road. A shape appears to grow out of the earth. Ominous and threatening. Moving closer all the time. And heading directly towards camera.

It is a jet-black Range Rover. A sinister machine slippery with heat. A change of angle explodes it into massive close up. Sunlight shunts in into stark silhouette and turns its blackened windows into chrome. Its invisible driver infects it with menace. Moving fast into a flow of traffic. On a motorway now. And overtaking everything in its path.

37. INT. RANGE ROVER. MOTORWAY. DAY.
Anyone who listens to this music will know where it cuts. Its powerful and foreboding optimism works in counterpoint to the image. BAGLEY *is at the wheel basking in sound. The interior is hi-tech leather. Black as his suit. Elegant gold cufflinks and got the eye drops in.*

Plus an important change to his appearance. He's retained the moustache. It's no longer the Edwardian span cultivated by his predecessor. But a neat brush like a luxury Hitler. The only other thing out of place is the bandages circling his neck. And even these are not so bad. Judging by the size of the lump the BOIL *has reduced considerably.* BAGLEY *momentarily removes his cigarette to reach for the phone. Hits a set of numbers and the call connects. He turns the tape down.*

BAGLEY (*phone*): John? Bagley. I wanna see you. No, outside.
Fine. Make it the bar across the street. I'll be there in
fifteen minutes.
He junks the phone and winds the volume. Big bass reverberates through the Rover. An inhalation becomes a smile. BAGLEY *is coming back!*

38. INT. WINE BAR. CITY. DAY.
One of those upmarket sawdust on the floor dives where they sling up a few barrels and charge you the price of a bottle for a single drink. Edith Piaf warbles in the background. Some pin-striped TWAT *behind the bar pumps a de-corking machine. The place is divided into booths where the quiche is going down. A* GIRL *collects a bottle from the* TWAT *and walks it to a table occupied by* BAGLEY *and* BRISTOL.

BRISTOL: Good to see you looking so good.
BAGLEY: Good to be feeling so good.

178

And the glasses are filled and they toast BAGLEY's *next sentence.*

Good to be coming back.

BRISTOL: Julia said it was gonna be at least another fortnight?

BAGLEY: Head swiveller says I'm fine.

His employer smiles like he's just had a new battery in the pacemaker.

It was just a coupla fuses blew. Stitches coming out in a week.

BRISTOL *refills both their glasses.* BAGLEY *lights another cigarette.*

Listen, I wanted to talk to you outside the office, ' cause I wanted a word about Harry. I don't wanna say anything bad about Harry, he's a good old pro. But what in Chrissame did you put him on the pimple cream for?

BRISTOL: Because you were off it. And it's all we could do to persuade them to wait.

BAGLEY: We're gonna have to persuade them to wait again.

BRISTOL: What d'you mean? We can't.

BAGLEY: We have to. Have you seen the presentation?

BRISTOL: No.

BAGLEY: I went in last night and took a look at it.

BRISTOL: What's he got?

BAGLEY: I don't wanna say anything bad about Harry.

BRISTOL: What's he got, Bagley?

How can BAGLEY *best put this? How can one describe such an old hat?*

BAGLEY: It's a U2. A totally depressed youth loiters in a disco. Close up. Face like a mapa the moon. Friends succeed while he fails to get the girl. Fade in a twelve-piece choir singing about love and acne.

BAGLEY *is having problems keeping his cynicism this side of yawning.*

Cut to the bathroom scene. The youth bastes his maculas. Close up of the product. The choir comes back chanting about hope. Back to the discotheque. The girl's still

dancing. Suddenly she spots the youth *without* his
pimples. They dance for three seconds, featuring her tits.
The choir reaches a crescendo. Feature the youth's
high-lighted dimples, and fade out (with a tasteful
suggestion of imminent fornication).

BRISTOL: What's the matter with that?

BAGLEY: Everything. I hate it. I've seen it a hundred times
before. In my opinion it'll grab us less than seven per cent
of the market.

BRISTOL: That's about the best you're gonna do. Seven or
eight, ten maximum.

BAGLEY *puts in a pause before his reply. His eyes alight with
energy.*

BAGLEY: I want *fifty*. And I know how to get it.

39. INT. CONFERENCE/SCREENING ROOM. ADVERTISING
AGENCY.

*A sales pitch is mounted at one end of the conference table. It is
basically a storyboard of the ad Bagley has already described. It is
accompanied by another display to which a sample of pimple cream
is attached. The product has acquired a name. 'The Final
Solution.'*

The man who choreographed the campaign is sitting next to
BRISTOL *at the far end of the table. He's a shagged-looking forty
year old named* HARRY WAX. BAGLEY *paces near the
presentation. Bristling with caffeine and full of smoke. There's no
question about it* BAGLEY *is back with a vengeance.*

BAGLEY: Before I get into my approach, I wanna warn you, at
first it might sound ridiculous. It's radical, and not
without its risks, but I'm certain I can pull it off. What it
is is Lawrence of Arabia, and a little town called Aqaba.
WAX *looks across at* BRISTOL. *What the fuck's this gotta do
with acne?*
The last thing they expected was for Lawrence to roar
across the desert and attack them from behind. It seemed
impossible. And because it was impossible all their
defences faced the wrong way.

*Now he's smiling down the table and two blank faces are
staring back.*

BAGLEY: And that's how I wanna sell this pimple cream. I
wanna come in from behind where they least expect me.
Just like Lawrence of Arabia.

At least he's not saying he's Napoleon. WAX *is still looking at*
BRISTOL. *Clearly from his expression he thinks* BAGLEY *will
have to spend a lot more dough at his psychiatrist's.* BAGLEY
*ignores the silence and turns attention to the display. He
removes the sample tube of cream.*

Now, as I see it, we've gotta forget this for at least three
months. I estimate that as the very minimum we need to
create the ravenous market I'm after.

He sticks the tube in his top pocket. WAX's *tone is somewhat
cynical.*

HARRY WAX: And how will you do that?

BAGLEY: By glamorising boils.

*The kind of silence that comes from a pair of partially open
mouths.*

BRISTOL: Glamorise them?

BAGLEY: That's right. I wanna make them fashionable. I
wanna encourage every kid to take a pride in his
break-outs. I wanna sell them the idea that boils are
'beautiful'. If I can do that, I can treble the market at a
minimum.

HARRY WAX: That's absurd.

BAGLEY: If you wanna sell 'em atom bombs you gotta sell 'em
fear. If we wanna sell this pimple cream, we gotta
encourage pimples.

WAX *looks vacant and so does* BRISTOL. *They both say*
'How?' *in unison.*

BAGLEY: This is how I see it. Every bit of market research
points to one simple fact. And that is the group in
possession of the biggest number of boils are the group
who buy the biggest number of records. But until
relatively recently pop music has been what you might call
anti-realism, which naturally implies anti-acne. But

181

suddenly there's a 'new wave'. They're out of work and they're angry. The kids are rejecting the 'glossy bullshit' and looking round for something different.

HARRY WAX: What's this gotta do with boils?

BAGLEY: I want that 'something different' to be pro-boil. All we gotta do is create our own group. A filthy bunch of bastards. We could even call them 'A Filthy Bunch of Bastards', or 'The Dog Shits', something like that.

BRISTOL: 'The Dog Shits'?

BAGLEY: Whatever, it's not important at the moment. The only vital thing is that they're a mess. They'll never wash. Openly reject all preconceptions of cleanliness and hygiene. They'll be covered in blackheads and *proud of it* – in fact, they'll have every juvenile skin complaint in the book. Then we do a heavy promotion. We buy them in and they have a hit. The kids identify with them and suddenly acne is desirable.

BRISTOL *and* WAX *look decidedly uneasy. And* BAGLEY *is looking at them.*

What d'you think?

HARRY WAX: Well, to be perfectly frank, Bagley, I've never heard such insane goat's shit in my life. Nobody in their right mind is going to desire acne.

BAGLEY: Of course they will. They'll desire anything they're told to desire. Nobody desires four hundred thousand tons of sulphur dioxide in the air, but they put up with it gladly, because they desire cars.

BRISTOL: We're talking about boils, Bagley.

BAGLEY: We're talking about anything we decide to sell them. If you'd come to me ten years ago, and said sell 'em toilet chains to hang on their backs and nuts and bolts to shove up their noses, I'd have said it was impossible. But they did it of their own free will. They had bald heads and green hair. Don't tell me I can't get out there and sell em boils to go with it.

HARRY WAX: It's crazy.

BAGLEY: It can't fail. If you were covered in pimples you'd

jump at it. No longer an outsider, you'd suddenly *belong*. People with afflictions always herd together – look at the Tories – it's an instinct. And in this case you get the added bonus of rejecting the values of a despicable establishment.

BAGLEY's *enthusiasm is having a positive effect on* BRISTOL. *His eyes are animated and close on his number one man as he moves quickly up the room. Suddenly the concept doesn't sound as absurd as he thought.*

Think of the spin-offs. Think of deodorants.

HARRY WAX: No TV company would touch them. You'd never get them on the screen.

BAGLEY: I wouldn't care if I didn't. It would reinforce their position. We'd bill them as refusing to be party to a corrupting media. They'd be brave rejecters of a vile dictator that has exploited youth and kept them all ashamed. (*He smiles.*) Plus I'd go video.

BRISTOL *is definitely intrigued and for a moment he stares into air.*

OK, it's in its infancy, and I know I haven't focused the geography yet. But I know I'm into something incredible here.

BRISTOL *gets his eyes back in order and reluctantly shakes his head.*

BRISTOL: We'd never sell it to the clients.

BAGLEY: There's nothing to sell. All we have to do is persuade them to wait while I create their market. As soon as the kids are riddled, we'll kill the group, re-introduce purity, and motor in with the cream. Except by then it'll be much bigger than that. It'll be an 'Adventure in Hygiene'.

For a second it looks as if BRISTOL *is going to remove his dentures. But the manipulation of his lips becomes a huge and astonished grin.*

BRISTOL: By Christ. It's marvellous.

HARRY WAX: You're not serious? It's absolutely ridiculous. Not only that it completely violates all accepted codes of advertising.

BAGLEY: Nonsense, the growth of boils is entirely natural.
Advertising doesn't come into it.

HARRY WAX: They'll have you in court for unfair practice.

BAGLEY: Who's gonna know?

HARRY WAX: I do. I do.

BAGLEY: May I remind you that you once sold sixty tons of
Phenol-contaminated sand as a 'Trash-Can Deodorant'?
And shall I remind you how much the Army paid you to
cart it away? And what you packaged and subsequently
sold it for?

That'll do to shut HARRY's *trap.* BRISTOL *opens his and is
reflective.*

BRISTOL: He's right, of course. Morally it stinks.

HARRY WAX: Of course it does. It's totally unethical.

BRISTOL: Totally. Totally.

40. INT. SOUND STAGE. FILM STUDIOS.

*Rock and roll! Try and get louder than this? Several cameras in
action including one tracking on a fifty-foot crane. Everything zeros
on the stage. Saxophone and electric guitars, plus a massive church
organ. Vandalised and smeared with graffiti. Maybe these are 'The
Dog Shits'? This almost certainly is* PHILLIS BLOKEY!

*She's a lot to describe. But her voice dominates everything. And
it is an amazing voice. She screams out a Who classic. 'Talkin'
'Bout My Generation.' Now let's talk about* PHILLIS. *Joe Cocker
has had a sex change. She's nineteen years old and big as a house.
Spew-coloured hair and a face like a wrestler. But Christ can the
ugly bitch sing!*

BAGLEY *listens via a pair of cans. Shirt sleeves and braces and
several yards of spiral lead connecting him to a bank of TV
monitors.* RICHARD *stands here wide-eyed at what he's looking at.*
PHILLIS *waddles forward with her legs barging together like
Torville and Dean.*

RICHARD: Christ.

He looks over at BAGLEY *who seems in some sort of ecstasy.*
PHILLIS *swivels and tears her mac down to reveal a yellow
bra strap like a girder to keep her shoulder blades apart. Her*

*back is a war zone of acne. A huge flyblown Madonna with a
bra like a pair of buckets!*

The crane puts six close ups of PHILLIS *on the monitors.*
BAGLEY *is here to greet them. He raises eyes towards*
RICHARD *who taps at his watch. 'Gotta go, Bagley.'*
BAGLEY *nods and then suddenly remembers.*

BAGLEY: Oh, Richard. You free Saturday?

RICHARD: Uh huh . . .

BAGLEY: Julia's putting a little party together. It's our
anniversary. And if you like, we'd love you along.
*He'd love to. Also love to get out of here. As he does the
organist insults music. And* PHILLIS *jives up the stage in an
orgasm of sound.*

41. INT. DRAWING ROOM. THE BAGLEY HOUSE. NIGHT.
The room is large and lovely and probably designed by JULIA
*herself. If she has a career this is probably it. She sits at an antique
table surrounded by Polaroid snaps and coloured pencils. There are
several fabric-sample books in use. Midway through sketching an
interior she hears a car. Looks up as a pair of headlights sweep the
windows. The pencil is thrown aside and instantly she's in mild
panic.*

*Carting her glasses off she rushes at the TV. Switches it on
willing the thing to hurry. It comes up with an ancient black and
white movie and that will apparently do. Kicking off shoes she
slumps on the sofa fabricating a pose that suggests she's been here
for hours.*

One second later BAGLEY *motors in looking exhausted but very
pleased with himself. Sports a smile and fresh set of bandages.
Doesn't seem to notice that his wife is brittle with artificial
relaxation. He fixes a whisky and she speaks without tearing eyes
from the TV.*

JULIA: How'd it go?

BAGLEY: Triffic. She's gonna be triffic.

JULIA: The *stitches*?

BAGLEY: Terrific. Didn't feel a thing.

He leans over the sofa and kisses the side of her head. JULIA *keeps eyes riveted to the TV.* BAGLEY *is feeling amorous and she knows it.*

Coming up to bed, darling?

JULIA: In a bit. I'm watching this. It's fascinating.

BAGLEY: What is it?

JULIA: Thriller.

BAGLEY: Well, don't be too long, because I'm practically dead.

He dumps his glass on the way out. And Santa comes down the chimney.

42. INT. BEDROOM. HOUSE. NIGHT.

Moonlight spills over the bed. BAGLEY *and* JULIA *are asleep. The camera creeps across the carpet like an intruder. As it approaches the bed a minute voice whispers 'Julia. Julia.' And* JULIA *finally wakes.*

At least she probably wakes. Turns towards BAGLEY *wondering what he wants. But her husband's snoring his head off. 'Julia. Julia.' This must be a dream because the voice is coming from the bandages. This must be a nightmare because a tiny tongue waggles through the gauze.*

BOIL: Julia. Julia.

The adrenalin squirts in with a sting of music. It has a terrifying resonance. Manufactured somewhere in the black recesses of her fear. Most of the face is hidden in bandages. She gasps at a little mouth.

Don't scream, darling. Don't scream.

She tries to scream but nothing emerges. Tries to escape but is paralysed in horror. Nothing moves but the camera. It climbs above her and looks directly down. The mini-mouth keeps talking and she keeps listening. But what it says can't be heard. The frightful music has intensified smothering all other sound. Meanwhile the camera begins to levitate above the bed. As it climbs focus pulls on JULIA's *face. She remains in close up while everything around distorts into black.*

43. INT. MARQUEE. THE BAGLEY HOUSE. EVENING.

The marquee is connected to the house via the drawing room's french windows. Everything is excessively pretty. The tent itself is yellow candy-striped canvas. There are yards and yards of yellow ribbon and gushes of yellow flowers. The floor is polished wood with a little stage at one end. A dozen tables surround the dance floor. More flowers on top of them clustered around as yet unlit yellow candles.

JULIA *has gone to town in here. Right now she's going round the tables with place names. She wears a tight black frock and has got the jewels on. She seems decidedly flustered. But that might be because of the amount of organising involved.* BAGLEY *appears with a plastic trash can. Dumps ice into an antique tin bath bursting with magnums of Cristal champagne. Still in pullover and corduroys. She tells him to hurry because it's getting late. Instead he comes across and she turns to fluster flowers. Can't avoid arms circling her from behind.*

BAGLEY: I didn't know you'd invited Penny.

JULIA: Of course I invited Penny. And you better be nice 'cause she's my friend.

BAGLEY: Poor Penny. I'm surprised she'd come. I suppose she does it out of some sort of social duty, like organising Dutch caps for the Hindus.

JULIA: It's nearly eight. Hurry up.

BAGLEY: There's just this little bit of neck here I need to kiss.

And he kisses the back of her neck. Nothing flinches but her pupils. PENNY *pretends not to notice as she passes. She carries a vast cauldron of water ice destined to join the magnificent buffet on display.* BAGLEY *presses something into* JULIA's *hand and smiles over at* PENNY.

BAGLEY: You're looking very summery, Penny.

PENNY: Thank you. It's a Marjeau . . . made in India.

JULIA *has opened the little case. Inside is a 300-volt emerald ring.*

BAGLEY: Happy anniversary, darling.

Before she can thank him he vanishes into the house. PENNY *wades across for a squint at the rock. Her question comes immediately after.*

PENNY: Are you having an affair, Julia?

JULIA: No.

PENNY: Then what's up?

JULIA: I don't know. I'm just so wound up about Dennis. I'm terrified his *thing*'ll start talking again.

PENNY: Well, it hasn't, has it?

JULIA: Not exactly . . .

She tries to find herself a smile. Comes up with a whisper instead.

. . . but I had this terrible, terrible dream, Penny . . . a nightmare, and I can't get it out of my head.

MRS WALLACE *appears togged in the white apron with the black dress. Apparently the musicians have arrived.* JULIA *replies (in brackets).*

(Tell them to come in, Silvia, do whatever they like.) We can't talk here. Come and have a drink.

44. INT. STUDY. HOUSE. EVENING.

Outside in the hall the grandfather clock strikes eight. PENNY *crushes a couch while* JULIA *patrols the rug. Both have a whisky on the rocks.*

JULIA: It said, Dennis wasn't my husband. It said, *it* was. And it said it with this horrible sort of, mouth. It said, he's an 'incarnation' of evil with a briefcase. Kept going on about a briefcase. Then it said zero five hundred again and again and again.

PENNY: What's zero five hundred?

JULIA: 'Cept horrendous, I don't know.

PENNY: And that's it?

JULIA: No. Then it told me to get the electric carving knife and cut his head off. It's *not* funny, Penny. It was the most terrifying experience of my life. So real, it could have been real.

PENNY: Have you told Dennis?

JULIA: Of course not. Last thing I wanna do is excite him. I tell you, Penny, I'm still waiting to scream about it.

PENNY *finishes her Scotch in a fat gulp and stands offering a hand.*

PENNY: Come along.

JULIA: Along where?

PENNY: We're going to look in the case.

JULIA: Oh, don't be so silly, Dennis doesn't even have a briefcase. He loathes them. Keeps everything in an old doctor's bag.

PENNY: Then with all due respect, Julia, I hardly see *I* should be the one accused of being silly. It's *you* that's had the silly dream. And quite honestly, under the circumstances I'm surprised you get to sleep at all. I personally would be up all night with a revolver.

JULIA: It's not just the dream, Penny.

Her pacing has taken her back to the bottles and she pours another.

Since Dennis came out of hospital, he's been peculiar. Sexually.

The beans are about to be spilt. PENNY *knows it and remains silent.*

He's obsessed with blackheads and fucking. Though not in that order.

PENNY: But you've always adored fucking.

JULIA: Not when I'm cleaning my teeth I don't. Not when I'm doing anything I don't. Truth is, Penny, I can't bear him touching me. I don't know why, but I can't. And I'm running out of headaches. He's absolutely sex mad. Tuesday shopping, he said, he wished I had nipples on my ass.

PENNY: Don't.

JULIA: And that's just the least of it.

The car coming up the drive arrives. Sounds of activity at the door.

Oh, Lord, they're arriving. Tell you about it later. And you breathe a word of this to anyone, Penny, and I'll absolutely kill you.

She opens the door on to the hall. RICHARD *is handing his mac over to* WALLACE *who works the cloaks. Both he and his date are sporting evenings.* RICHARD *barely has time for a smile before he disappears.*

RICHARD: Dying for a pee. This is Monica.

MONICA *is a bit of a gummy job with reddish hair. But she's pretty enough for Richard. She collects the cloak tags and* PENNY *introduces herself. A handshake later they're heading for the drawing room.*

45. INT. DRAWING ROOM. HOUSE. EVENING.

The musicians run a sound check in the marquee. Plus one or two professional-looking caterers about. MONICA *conducts a brief admiring tour of the décor while* JULIA *fixes drinks. Maybe a bit of improvised chat of the 'How long have you been married?' variety. If so the answer's seven years. Everyone gets a sherry on ice. The glasses go up with a* 'Happy Anniversary'. MONICA *smiles and* JULIA *says* 'Snap!'

JULIA: You're wearing 'Le De'. Givenchy.

She pokes a wrist at MONICA's *nose as evidence she's wearing it too.*

It's my totally favourite scent, and they've stopped making it.

MONICA: Have they? I bought it in Marbella.

JULIA: Well, you're lucky. It's extinct.

Further details are terminated by the arrival of RICHARD. *A bit of fake embarrassment to be the first. But he'll have a whisky and soda. While* PENNY *dispenses it* JULIA *floats in manufacturing an anaesthetic smile. Taking* RICHARD's *hand she guides him to the nearest sofa.*

JULIA: Richard, darling, can I just get something over with, then we can all forget it? Thing is, I didn't really want to have this party. I thought we might be rushing it. But Dennis's psychiatrist thinks it's a good idea to get him back into the swim as soon as possible.

RICHARD: He's all right, isn't he? I've never seen him on such good form.

JULIA: Oh, absolutely, he's fine. But he's just had his stitches out, so naturally, we're all a little bit apprehensive. So, if anything happens, which I'm certain it won't, the rule is we all sort of go along with it.

PENNY: We 'humour him'. Discreetly.

JULIA: Not exactly, Penny. We just behave normally. I don't want him excited, certainly don't want any arguments.

MONICA: What's the matter with him?

JULIA: He was overworked and nearly had a breakdown. But he's much better now.

46. INT. BATHROOM. HOUSE. EVENING.

BAGLEY *is in front of the bathroom mirror. Bandages off and lathering up to shave. He uses expensive but traditional equipment. Ivory and badger brush. Ivory and gold cut-throat razor. A cigar returns to his mouth and his eyes are attracted to the* BOIL. *At least what is left of it. It's of similar colour and about the size of a small mushroom. Though no mushroom could look so ill. Its mouth is scarred with neat little stitch marks like a split seam in a rugby ball. It remains silent and apparently inanimate. Satisfied it will stay that way he prepares his razor and stretches skin on his neck. His face suddenly clouds with concern. The* BOIL *manages to open an eye.*

BAGLEY: You're alive?

> *Indeed there's still life in it.* BAGLEY *slowly approaches the glass.*

> Can you speak?

> *Apparently not even though it tries. A bit of torture is irresistible.*

> You don't look at all well, you know. Not being a medical man, I wouldn't take my word for it, but I'd say you had the 'Mark'.

> *The* BOIL *watches him with loathing fermenting in its bloodshot eye.*

> You look like a doomed bollock.

BOIL: I want to speak to my wife.

BAGLEY: Oh, you can talk, can you?

BOIL: Let me speak to Julia, and I swear I'll never speak again.

BAGLEY: Speak to her of what, Boil?

BOIL: I want her to see my film. Please.

BAGLEY: Oh, so that's what's worrying you, is it? Well, let me put your mind at rest. First, on a purely ideological basis, it's out of the question. And second, I've burnt it.

BOIL: Oh no.

BAGLEY: Oh yes . . .

And he begins to shave with pleasure equal to the BOIL's *distress.*

And prepare yourself for another little fluctuation of blood-pressure, 'cause it's not the only thing I've burnt. I've also burnt Julia's diaphragm.

BOIL: Oh no.

BAGLEY: Oh yes . . .

Only the sound of bristles and blade. His grin is a detail of evil.

It's time Julia had a baby. Hopefully a baby Boible. And I'm gonna pump him with E numbers and emulsifiers. Rectifiers and stabilisers.

BOIL: Ogre.

BAGLEY: I'm gonna stuff him with preservatives right up to his little brim.

BOIL: You are a criminal ogre!

BAGLEY: It's all *quite normal*, Boil. Now, I intend to commence vigorous intercourse at about one a.m. I don't wanna go too far into the details of what this might mean, but if I was you I'd have an early night.

BOIL: Cut your throat monster! In the name of humanity. Cut your filthy throat!

BAGLEY: Don't start getting emotional.

BOIL: I'll do everything I can to harm you!

BAGLEY: You can't harm me, you miserable little bit of garbage. You'll be dead in a couple of days, so why don't you try and do it with some dignity?

BOIL: Dignity? You corruption! Julia! Julia!

Further protest is terminated as the bandages are tightly rewound.

BAGLEY: Shut your trap, Boil. And keep it shut.

47. INT. MARQUEE. HOUSE. NIGHT.

The place is filled with bow ties and lipstick and champagne going down and the candles are lit and yards of white fairy lights twinkle over the stage. Somewhere in this mess of mouths there must be a conversation. So why not listen to this one?

BRISTOL: Fifty per cent of politics is about creating a problem, and the other fifty per cent is about offering to solve it. All you gotta do is bugger something up then hasten round to your nearest TV station with a solution. Doesn't matter what it is, the environment, hospitals, crime – create a 'crime wave', and up will pop some perfectly plausible head selling police.

RICHARD: Bagley calls it the 'Old Rock through the Window Technique'.

PENNY looks like she smelt something she doesn't like the smell of.

BRISTOL: And that's exactly what it is.

PENNY: Well, it might work on everyone else, but it doesn't work on me.

BRISTOL: If you breathe *air* it works on you.

Already half ass-holed he shoves his glass at a retreating RICHARD.

Large one, no ice, please, Richard.

MONICA: But if you're all aware of it, how can you bear to work in an industry that perpetuates it?

BRISTOL: It's probably a defect from birth.

He sticks his pipe back into the grin and ambushes a passing JULIA.

Come and rescue me, I'm being attacked.

JULIA: Who's attacking you?

BRISTOL: Penelope here. She's telling me off because I think your husband's a genius.

PENNY: I simply think it's outrageous that Dennis should be

193

allowed to manipulate children's minds.

BRISTOL is tired of this dialogue. His eyes have already departed.

BRISTOL: There is the dear boy. Come along, I want to ask you both a question.

JULIA: No business, John. That's the rule.

And she takes the arm offered and they tramp away into the glitter. At the other side of the marquee BRISTOL embraces a radiant BAGLEY.

MONICA: Is that him? (*It is.*) He's very good looking.

PENNY: If you like that sort of thing.

RICHARD returns with Bristol's whisky. PENNY quickly reroutes him.

RICHARD: Come and meet Bagley, darling.

He takes off with purpose and the girls follow at a gossiping pace.

MONICA: Julia seems terribly tense.

PENNY: I'm not surprised. It's *him*.

She pumps eyes at BAGLEY who evaporates to greet someone else. His disappearance provides convenient space for a bit of light scandal.

He had an operation, and went weird in the 'bed department'.

MONICA: What d'you mean?

PENNY: Sex.

The word produces a facial muscle warp and a familiar kisser passes.

Hello, Basil.

BASIL: Hello, Penny. Lovely party.

PENNY: Super.

And now he's out the way PENNY gets back to conspiratorial business.

Apparently, he's insatiable.

MONICA: Really?

PENNY: Dick. Dick. Dick. Dick. Dick.

Her great breasts heave and MONICA gives them space as she moves in.

Shouldn't really be telling you this, it was said in the strictest of confidence, and that's exactly how I'm telling you. She said, he's got a permanent horn.

MONICA: Really?

PENNY: Said she's desperate. Other night he saw to her for an hour and a half. She finally got to sleep. Woke up fifteen minutes later and caught him down the bed with a huge black rubber torch.

MONICA: Torch?

PENNY: Flashlight.

MONICA: Doing what?

PENNY: *Scrutinising*. He was under the covers. Said he'd *lost* something. Contact lens. Said he didn't wanna wake her up. And unlucky for her that he did 'cause she got another hour's worth.

A voice scythes through the P/A silencing PENNY *and everyone else. All eyes on the stage now.* BAGLEY *is up there with the microphone.*

BAGLEY: Not gonna make a speech. I'd just like to thank you all for coming, and making our anniversary so special. And most of all I'd like to thank Julia for organising it all, and for being such a special wife.

A little bit of applause for this. Here comes a bit of an 'in' joke.

Judging by some of the streaming colds coming out of our downstairs bathroom, I don't suppose half of you could eat a thing. But for the other half that can, there's a few snacks here, so let feeding begin.

48. INT. MARQUEE. THE BAGLEY TABLE. NIGHT.
Everyone is midway chomping through the scoff. At this table a magnum of champagne is going down. BAGLEY *at one end and* JULIA *at the other. Their guests will get names if they get a line.*

BAGLEY *seems on sparkling form. Presently enjoying* JONATHAN's *toast to his evident health. While glasses are up* BAGLEY *proposes a toast of his own.*

BAGLEY: And I'd also like to propose a small snifter to our new star.

RICHARD: I thought she was coming.

BAGLEY: She is. She's been held up.

And he toasts 'To Phillis Blokey' *and* RICHARD *elucidates for* MONICA.

RICHARD: She's the singer with the boils.

BAGLEY: To boils, acne and blackheads.

This one's accepted with reluctance but everyone raises their glass.

JONATHAN: Whass this cream gonna be called?

BAGLEY: I dunno yet. Right now we're stuck with Filthy Harry's Final Solution.

JULIA: Who's 'Filthy Harry'?

BAGLEY: You know Harry Wax. Creative.

BRISTOL: Only man here in a hired suit.

BAGLEY: Eyes as close as a Doberman's balls. But I don't wanna say anything bad about Harry.

JULIA: Then don't.

JONATHAN's *girlfriend is a very cute blonde with a size four brain.*

JENNIFER: I don't think anyone would ever encourage me to grow boils.

JULIA *shoots her a look like a kick in the shins. If she wasn't so distant it would be practical. She also tries to change the subject.*

JULIA: How's the new book coming along, Penny?

But she's too late because BAGLEY *has already moved in on* JENNIFER. *His expression is about 40 per cent champagne and 60 per cent conceit.*

BAGLEY: You're not the market I'm after, darling. But if you were, I would. I could sell you anything from a boil to a hydrogen bomb.

JENNIFER: I don't think so. I'm anti-nuke.

BAGLEY: Shall I tell you why people buy hydrogen bombs? Because they're not like the bombs people used to use in wars. We put an 'added ingredient' into bombs these

196

days. It's called 'peace'. Our warheads are stuffed to the brim with it. And we're years ahead of the competition, of course, because the Russians don't put any peace in theirs.

BRISTOL *laughs*.

BRISTOL: Very good, Bagley.

JULIA (*hard at Bristol*): Can anyone think of a discreet way of changing the subject?

BRISTOL: I'm sorry, Julia, but I'm afraid Dennis is absolutely right. There's a splendid example of what he's talking about outside our building. Ever looked at it?

JULIA: Can't say as I have . . .

BRISTOL: Well, there's an obelisk there to the glory of the Royal Marines. And there's a plaque depicting a Marine shoving his bayonet into a Chinaman's gut. And he's so shocked, his pigtail's sticking-up like an exclamation mark. Underneath it says, 'Shanghai Campaign, 1898'.

JULIA: Would you pass the pepper please, Penny?

BRISTOL: Imagine seeing that in Peking? A plaque of a Chinaman pumping his bayonet into an Englishman half-way up Regent Street? A bowler hat levitating in shock. And underneath, 'West London Campaign, 1898'.

BAGLEY *laughs*.

JULIA: Pepper please, Penny.

Gnashing continues and JONATHAN *manages to find a change of subject.*

PENNY: This is excellent.

JONATHAN: Yes, I was about to say, I notice Penny's gone carnivorous.

JULIA: She lacked protein.

PENNY: And minerals. I couldn't get all I needed out of normal greenstuff.

BOIL: There's a lawn out the back. Why don't you shove out for a graze?

All heads turn in BAGLEY's *direction. For a moment it seems some explanation is forthcoming but he's silent.* BAGLEY's

197

eyes finally contact the offended party. With superhuman effort PENNY *responds with a smile. It unrolls along her mouth like the opening of a stiff zip.*

PENNY: That's quite funny.

BAGLEY: A joke. Just a joke.

And he grins at her while winding his bandages tighter over the BOIL.

You were gonna tell us about your new book?

JONATHAN: What's it called, Penny?

PENNY: *The Contexturalisation of Contemporary Feminism.*

JONATHAN: Really? What's it about?

BOIL: Boeuf Bourguignon and periods.

BAGLEY *boggles over his napkin like a paranoid Bedouin in a yashmak. His bandages are now pulled so tightly his eyes are beginning to bulge.*

BRISTOL: You don't think the bandages may be a little on the tight side, Bagley?

BAGLEY: No. Perfect. Thank you.

BOIL: Julia, Julia.

JULIA: Are you all right, darling?

BAGLEY: Marvellous.

Crisp with fury he stands and smiles and moves away from the table.

Would you excuse me for a moment?

PENNY *takes advantage of the hiatus to squeeze a whisper at* MONICA.

PENNY: I tell you, he's absolutely barking.

49. INT. BATHROOM. HOUSE. NIGHT.

Purple of face and furious of eye BAGLEY *explodes into the bathroom. Seething with rage towards the lump he gasps as he releases the bandage. Also releases a tirade of venom from the suffocating feruncle.*

BAGLEY: Shut up, you little moron. I'd like to wring your bastard neck.

BOIL: Do it, then. Do it. Put me out of my misery.

BAGLEY: Oh, no, not yet, you unwholesome pustule. I want

198

you to live just a bit longer. I want you around, *tonight* when the shagging begins!

Before the BOIL *can protest* BAGLEY *shoves a tube of household glue into his victim's mouth. It splutters rapidly into silence.*

Tasty, is it? Here, have another suck! Let's hear you squawk now!

50. INT. STAGE/MARQUEE. HOUSE. NIGHT.

The party has matured. Just candles and fairy lights now.
PHILLIS BLOKEY *is on stage. Her frock shimmers with tinsel. She stands totally still leaning over the mike. A cigarette between fingers with smoke drifting into the lights. It's appropriate for the tune. She sings 'Smoke Gets in Your Eyes'. Occasionally takes a deep drag on the fag between phrases.* PHILLIS *could do it standing on her head.*

BAGLEY *is among the few faces watching. But the majority of guests are vacillating on and off the dance floor. And a dance isn't a bad idea. He turns and navigates a haphazard course looking for* JULIA.

JULIA *is discovered chattering with a variety of kissers including* RICHARD *and* BASIL *and* MONICA. BAGLEY's *invitation for her to dance is resisted with a shake of the head.* 'Come on, Julia.' *If she makes an excuse it's drowned in the general din.* BAGLEY *redirects his hand at* MONICA. *But she doesn't want to dance either.* 'Come along. *I insist.' And* RICHARD *insists too.* 'Go on. It's his anniversary.'

Reluctantly MONICA *is brought to her feet. (The mechanics of what's happened might need explanation.* BAGLEY's *invitation will be staged in such a way that the* BOIL *will think* BAGLEY *is dancing with* JULIA.)

And as soon as MONICA *is in* BAGLEY's *arms the* BOIL *is certain he's dancing with* JULIA. *A sound of sniffing under the gauze as the* BOIL *recognises the Givenchy.* MONICA *does her best to suppress her tension. Finds a bit of a gummy smile as her partner manoeuvres closer.*

MONICA: Have you got a cold too?

BAGLEY: Not my drug.

She is re-absorbed into his embrace and she hears the sniffing again.

BAGLEY: I know that smell. 'Le De.'

MONICA: You don't have to hold me quite so tightly, Dennis.

BAGLEY: Sorry, 'fraid the 'clinch' is the only dance I know.

During this exchange their heads swap position. MONICA *is now Boilside. Pressure from* BAGLEY *all but forces her ear into the bandage.*

BOIL: Oh, Julia. Julia, darling.

Her eyes widen at the intense whisper. She's convinced it's BAGLEY.

MONICA: Monica.

BAGLEY: I know.

For a moment the heads are separated. And now come together again.

BOIL: Julia.

MONICA *comes up with the sort of smile more usually associated with a dog fucking your leg in public. Many variables compete for her expression. There is a desire to flee. There is panic at exciting him.*

Please don't scream, or pull away, we might never get this chance again. It's difficult for me to talk because my sinuses are full of glue.

BAGLEY'*s hands wander over her shoulders and* PHILLIS *keeps singing.*

BAGLEY: You're not wearing a bra?

MONICA: Not really.

A sound like Satan clearing his throat. It is the BOIL *clearing its.*

BOIL: I love you. I love you madly. And this isn't a dream, it's reality.

MONICA *is only too aware of it. The grimace has paralysed her chops.* BAGLEY *runs fingers down her back. Is obviously enjoying the clinch.*

BOIL: Don't speak. Just listen. I'm desperate. You're gonna need a condom, and quick. The fucking's gonna start in

about an hour. And believe me, you're gonna have a
monster on top of you.
*Unquestionably she believes him. Passing dancers have
become a blur.*
Last thing in the world I want is you pregnant. Christ, it's
gonna be a nightmare in bed with you. I don't know what
I'm gonna do. I've got one last desperate hope. And I
know it's a fantasy. But I'd like you to lash out with a
knife while you're fucking.
MONICA: Ahhh!!! Stay away from me! Keep away!
*The bubble has burst. Or rather the rock has hit the pool.
MONICA backs off as if she's dealing with a rabid dog. The
dancers kaleidoscope into a sort of cordon around her.
BAGLEY stares like a nut.*
BAGLEY: Has that bastard been whispering to you?
*She doesn't answer but beats it fast for the house. BAGLEY
punches at his neck. 'Bastard. Bastard.' And those that must
follow MONICA.*

51. INT. HALLWAY. HOUSE. NIGHT.
MONICA *leads the convoy and is clearly upset.* RICHARD *and*
JULIA *in her wake. The latter wants to know what's going on. She
gets a garbled account on the hoof climaxing as the cloak tags are
handed in.*
MONICA: I'm sorry, Julia, but I think your husband's
completely bananas. Going along with someone isn't the
same as listening to a tirade of obscenity.
JULIA: What did he say?
MONICA: I can't tell you.
She grabs coats and hands one to RICHARD. *A briefcase
comes across.*
RICHARD: I'm sorry, Julia. Lovely party.
His attempt to be polite is fractured by MONICA's *haste to get
out.*
JULIA: Richard. Your case.
RICHARD: Oh, that isn't mine. It belongs to Bagley. He left it
at the studios.

Shock one is the front door. Shock two is the chill in JULIA's
face. Shock three is BAGLEY's *eyes alternating between*
JULIA *and the case.*

52. INT. BEDROOM. HOUSE. NIGHT.

Just coming up to four-thirty on the bedside clock. JULIA *stares at
the revolving second hand. Her expression suggests she's been
staring at it for ages (while waiting for* BAGLEY *to sleep?). A
promising-sounding snore develops. With a mix of caution and
apprehension she turns towards him. He lies flat on his back and
appears to be fast asleep.*

JULIA's *mouth leads the way in. At first it seems she will kiss
him. Instead she gears herself up to whisper at the* BOIL. *But how
should she address it? She finally settles on the logical title and
barely articulates* 'Boil? Boil?' *Her terror of waking* BAGLEY
*keeps the volume low. She tries again without success and recoils
back in dread. Is* BAGLEY *waking up? (No he's merely turning in
his sleep.) But the* BOIL *is now downside in the bedclothes and
incapable of hearing her.*

53. INT. (ANOTHER ANGLE). BEDROOM. NIGHT.

JULIA *is crawling across the floor towards the bed. She is equipped
with the hose from the vacuum cleaner. It wears a long thin nozzle
of the type used to plunge down the sides of chairs. With ultimate
caution she inserts the device under* BAGLEY's *neck seeking contact
with the* BOIL. *On knees now with her primitive 'phone' in
position. She hardly has air for the whisper. But here it comes.*
'Boil. Boil.'

*And the end of the tube is transferred to her ear. Fright-eyed she
listens to the silence. (Almost praying the silence will be
maintained.) She's poised for another try when once again her
husband shifts in slumber. Her terror settles and she presses lips to
the tube.* 'Can you hear me, Boil?' *A slug of black electricity hits
her eyes. She is obviously getting a reply!* 'Where has he hidden
the briefcase?' *No one can hear but* JULIA. *But she's hearing a
voice down the line!*

54. INT. GARAGE. HOUSE. NIGHT.

A light goes on, revealing a large double garage. It contains a red Ferrari and the black Range Rover. In dressing gown and slippers JULIA *approaches the latter. On its rear window is one of those dreadful slogans with a heart substituting for the word love. The slogan is* I LOVE BOILS. JULIA *opens the back door and moves an old raincoat aside. Underneath is a gleaming leather Dunhill briefcase.*

Everything shifts into close up. Close on her eyes as she stares at the case. Close on its brass combination locks. Closer still on the numbers tumbling round. Zero five hundred suddenly makes sense! She sets the first combination. And now the second. Her heart almost in her mouth as her thumbs slide at the catches. Both locks snap open! Jesus this is a nightmare. Except she knows she isn't dreaming. The case contains several 10 × 8s *of* PHILLIS *and a single video cassette.*

55. INT. STUDY. HOUSE. NIGHT.

Still in major close up on a video machine. Pulsing green numbers. Four thirty-seven a.m. The cassette is clicked into place. JULIA's *fingers start the recorder and the frame widens to include the TV.*

BAGLEY *comes up on screen. Cardboard box on his head. Lecturing into the camera. He looks more than somewhat barmy. But as yet there is no sound.* JULIA *finds the remote control and pushes up the volume. Because of the wine case on his head she can't hear the* BOIL. *Only what* BAGLEY *says is audible. It makes for a rather disjointed show.*

BAGLEY (*TV*): . . . there are millions and millions of
hamburgers, Julia. And if something isn't done to stop
them, they'll end up destroying us all.
The unheard interjections of the BOIL *produce a curious facial tick.*
Hamburgers are coming out of the rain forests in their
millions.
Circumstances dictate that he must articulate with crazy intensity.

Hamburgers are coming from Brazil.

And suddenly for no apparent reason BAGLEY's *emphasis goes berserk.*

Yes! Cheeseburgers too!

JULIA *stares at the TV in disbelief. And here comes a real beauty.*

Pork pies have nothing to do with it!

BAGLEY *almost knocks his box off. Attempts to control his emotions.*

BAGLEY: I had a nasty feeling I was gonna have to wake up to this.

JULIA *almost leaps out of her skin!* BAGLEY *is behind her in pyjamas.*

If I was you, I'd turn this off, Julia. It's only gonna upset you.

The desperate BAGLEY *on screen responds to this latest interference.*

BAGLEY (*TV*): You see what a nightmare I'm in? You see why I can't talk to you?

BAGLEY *looks at the television with a black but supercilious smile.*

BAGLEY: Who are you talking to then?

BAGLEY (*TV*): God, it *converses.* I'm talking to *it.*

JULIA *is staring in utter confusion.* BAGLEY *heads towards the booze.*

BAGLEY: I need a cigarette.

BAGLEY (*TV*): Be silent, you Moloch.

BAGLEY: Moloch?

And the word seems to amuse him. But he doesn't find any cigarettes.

BAGLEY (*TV*): Yes, yes, you, you Moloch. You bogy.

BAGLEY: Switch it off, darling.

BAGLEY (*TV*): No, please, I beg of you.

JULIA *watches as though hypnotised. And* BAGLEY *shrugs his shoulders.*

BAGLEY: If you insist we have to listen to this bullshit, I need a cigarette.

He heads for the door with the Scotch he just poured. JULIA *is still mesmerised by the television.* BAGLEY (*TV*) *is in process of doing his deal with the* BOIL *to get a cigarette. He will now also head for the door.*

BAGLEY (*TV*): Don't turn off, darling. Sixty seconds, and I'll be back.

> *It will be less than five seconds before* BAGLEY *is back. Meanwhile* JULIA *stares at an empty shot of the room she is sitting in. It is somehow appropriate to her mood. She is exhausted of everything except being. In he comes with a cigarette in his mouth and the pack in his hand. They look at each other, wondering who will talk first.*

BAGLEY: Penny said you had a bad dream.

JULIA: Did she? Well she shouldn't have.

BAGLEY: Said the Boil had spoken to you.

> JULIA *almost says 'It did.' But* BAGLEY *is moving in to reassure her.*

BAGLEY: It didn't. Believe me, it didn't.

JULIA: Told me where you'd hidden the case.

BAGLEY: It didn't. *I* told you where I'd *put* the briefcase. I didn't dare wake up and ask why you'd decided to vacuum clean me in the middle of the night.

> BAGLEY *is thinking on his feet. And that's something he excels at.*

I told you where I'd 'put' it, because I'm only too aware of the tension you've been trying to conceal.

> *He fixes another whisky and allows a little anguish into his voice.*

And painful though it is for me, I thought by letting you 'discover' the film, it might have a sort of therapeutic effect. There'd be no more secrets. Nothing left to hide. (*He tries to smile.*) I realise, of course, that was foolish.

JULIA: If the Boil didn't speak to me, how did I know the combination?

> *Here comes a major lie. If* JULIA *calls it* BAGLEY *is in deep trouble.*

BAGLEY: Because it's written up in the kitchen, it's been on

the bulletin board for weeks. You must have seen it two
hundred times.

JULIA: I've never noticed noticing it.

BAGLEY: It's on a red and white receipt. I'll go and get it if you
like.

Something collapses in JULIA's *eyes.* BAGLEY *regains new
confidence.*

I realise I've been very selfish. So busy thinking about the
stress I was under, I'd forgotten what a terrible time it's
been for you.

Both switch eyes back to the television screen as BAGLEY
(*TV*) *re-appears.*

BAGLEY: I really don't want you to watch this, darling. I
intended to burn it. It's only going to upset you.

JULIA: I'm already upset. Please be quiet.

BAGLEY (*TV*): Are you there? I pray you're there.

BAGLEY (*TV*) *moves close into the camera. Still wearing his
box but with an addition to the mad image. A cigarette pokes
out of the side of his neck and from time to time the* BOIL *will
exhale gusts of smoke.*

I've just seen you in the kitchen. I know you think I'm
crazy. But in a minute you'll see my film and you can
judge my 'madness' for yourself.

Also smoking BAGLEY *loiters on the carpet looking
increasingly uptight.*

Everything's assembled from my old ads. All I've done is
re-edit them, revoice them, and put in the *truth*.

The BOIL *blows a smoke ring as* BAGLEY (*TV*) *moves
forward to tap the lens.*

No truth ever gets out of here. They got this bastard by
the balls! Greed has installed its lackeys into the highest
offices in this land, and they're conducting a crimewave of
unprecedented ferocity. Anywhere you wanna look
they're at it. Oil companies sold as 'champions of the
environment'! Wild animals prancing through the
woodlands! Meanwhile the filth from their cars is wiping
out half the forests of Europe!

BAGLEY: I can't listen to any more of this.

BAGLEY (*TV*): You swore you'd be quiet!

BAGLEY: Yeah, but I'd forgotten what a nightmare you are.

BAGLEY (*TV*): I wanna be heard! I wanna be heard!

BAGLEY: I wanna drink.

BAGLEY (*TV*): Then get it yourself! Jesus, I forgotten what I
    was gonna say?

    BAGLEY *is back at the whisky bottle. Eyes to the TV with
    sarcasm.*

BAGLEY: I believe you were about to explain why hamburgers
    are going to be the cause of the Third World War.

BAGLEY (*TV*): That's right you cynical bastard.

BAGLEY: We're all ears.

JULIA: How can you argue with a television?

BAGLEY: Because this poor, sick, creature, with a box on his
    head was *me*. And I know exactly what I'm gonna say.
    And in demonstration the next phrase will be said by both
    BAGLEYS.

THE BAGLEYS: Destruction of the rain forests (by, amongst
    other things, hamburgers) is going to lead to a world
    commodity crisis, and the commodity will be *oxygen*.

BAGLEY: What mad bollocks . . .

BAGLEY (*TV*): It is not bollocks! They're turning the rain
    forests into deserts. Within twenty-five years the
    Brazilians'll be 'fixing' world oxygen prices, in exactly the
    same way as the Arabs 'fix' the price for oil.

BAGLEY: No more.

BAGLEY (*TV*): You want the air? You pay for it!

BAGLEY: No more.

    He grabs the remote control and freeze-frames BAGLEY
    (*TV*). *The 'TV hater' has been reduced to one himself and
    shares all attendant risks.*

JULIA: Leave it on, Dennis. I wanna watch.

BAGLEY: I don't know how you can say that.

    *He turns on fake emotion worthy of anything in a Mike
    Winner film.*

    You know what it does to me? Reliving this nightmare?

Look at him. He's got a cigarette stuck in his bandages.
The man's mad.

JULIA: Why d'you keep calling him 'him'?

It's a fair point considering 'he' is 'him' and BAGLEY *isn't*
'him'.

It's you.

BAGLEY: All right, me. It's *me*, and I was *ill*. You were the one
that said so. You can't have it both ways, darling. You
said I needed help. And I got help. And now I'm better,
which is why I can't bear to watch this dreadful insanity.

JULIA: You still wanna sell them boils?

BAGLEY: Nothing crazy about *that*. It's a free market. People
will either buy, or they won't buy. Nobody's forcing
them. Everyone knows what they're getting.

JULIA: Perhaps they don't.

BAGLEY: Of course they do. People might be a bit greedy from
time to time, but we're not blind. We got our eyes open,
and we have a choice.

JULIA: Perhaps.

BAGLEY: Stop saying perhaps. What's 'perhaps' got to do with
it?

JULIA: Perhaps they don't.

BAGLEY: *'Perhaps'* if they'd hanged Jesus Christ, we'd all be
kneeling in front of a fucking gibbet! But that isn't the
real world. In the real world I have a *choice*. Do I want it,
or don't I? And in this case, I most certainly *do not*.

And he thrusts the remote at the TV and that is the end of
BAGLEY.

56. EXT. HILLSIDE. DAY.

Shove in a few church bells and you've got an ad for rural
England. BAGLEY *appears in the middle of it. Walks his dark*
horse up the sloping meadow. Divorce may be in the air but it
doesn't seem to bother him. Indeed, the bastard seems positively
elated. He swivels in the saddle and gets a dose of inspiration.

BAGLEY: And did those feet in ancient time Walk upon
England's mountains green?

208

Sounds like provincial Shakespeare. And now he's talking to himself.

The answer to that question is '*No*'. Jesus did *not* shuffle up the Weald of Kent. Can you hear me, Boil? No, I don't imagine you can. But you've got to admit, that's one of the most graceful pieces of propaganda this nation's ever produced. A magnificent blend of Christianity and Conservatism. And Conservatism is capitalism, and capitalism *sells*. Did Jesus land at Margate? Ah yes my Boil! For millions and millions of school kids, the answer to that question is '*Yes*'.

BAGLEY *continues talking to his* BOIL *puffed with self-satisfaction.*

And that's the difference between you and me, Boil. I was brought up to believe in that, and so should you. But you don't because you're a defeatist. You don't want Jerusalem, do you? You don't even want roads. God, I never want to go on another train as long as I live! Roads represent a fundamental right of man to have access to the good things in life. Without roads established family favourites would become élitist delicacies. Pota-soup would be for the few. There'd be no more tea bags. No instant potatoes. No long-life cream. There'd be no aerosols, detergents would vanish! So would tinned spaghetti, and baked beans with six frankfurters. The right to smoke one's chosen brand would be denied! Chewing gum would probably disappear. So would pork pies. Foot deodorisers would climax without hope of replacement. And when the hydrolised protein and monosodium glutamate reserves ran out food would rot in its packets. Jesus Christ, there wouldn't be any packets! Packaging would vanish from the face of the earth. But worst of all there'd be no more cars. And more than anything people *love* their cars. They have a right to them. If they have to sweat all day in some stinking factory making disposable cigarette lighters or everlasting Christmas trees, by Christ, they're *entitled* to them.

Working himself up and working his horse into a canter up the hill.

They're entitled to any innovation technology brings. Whether it's ten per cent *more* of it, or fifteen per cent *off* of it, they're entitled to it! They're entitled to one of four important new ingredients. Why should anyone have to clean their teeth without important new ingredients? Why the hell shouldn't they have their CZT? How *dare* some snotty Marxist carbuncle presume to deny them it!

And suddenly he's off his nag and struggling on foot to the crest of the hill like Henry II with something important on his mind.

They *love* their CZT. They want it. They need it. They positively adore it. And by Christ, while I've got air in my body, they're going to get it!

A splendid view from up here. The horizon encompasses five counties. A sort of plinth commemorates some past overseas mass murder. Probably the First World War. One side sports a relief carving of a crucifix with a point like a sword. Onward Christian Soldiers! It also has a conveniently flat top and BAGLEY *clambers up it. He stands and stares across the countryside like a dictator surveying his kingdom.*

They're gonna get it bigger, and brighter, and *better*. I'll put CZT in their margarine if necessary. Shove vitamins in their toilet rolls! If happiness means the *whole world* standing on a double layer of foot deodorisers, *I, Bagley*, will see they get them. I'll give them anything, and everything they want. By God, I will.

He turns a 365-degree circle. Before him is a panorama of unspoilt countryside. A superb and unending location on which roads and factories and advertising hoardings can be erected. BAGLEY's *arms open into a traditional Christlike pose. The sun flares behind his head.*

I shall not cease till Jerusalem is built on England's green and pleasant land.

BAGLEY	RICHARD E. GRANT
JULIA	RACHEL WARD
BRISTOL	RICHARD WILSON
PENNY WHEELSTOCK	JACQUELINE TONG
MENDLEBAUM	JOHN SHRAPNEL
MONICA	SUSAN WOOLDRIDGE
HARRY WAX	HUGH ARMSTRONG
RICHARD	MICK FORD
MAUD	JACQUELINE PEARCE
WAITER	CHRISTOPHER SIMON
WAITER	GINO MELVAZZI
TWEEDY MAN	VICTOR LUCAS
TWEEDY WOMAN	DAWN KEELER
GIRL IN ELEVATOR	KERRYANN WHITE
RECEPTIONIST	VIVIENNE MCKONE
BALD BUSINESSMAN	DONALD HOATH
NOT BALD BUSINESSMAN	JOHN LEVITT
PRIEST	GORDON GOSTELOW
JONATHAN	PIP TORRENS
BASIL	TONY SLATTERY
JENNIFER	RACHEL FIELDING
MRS WALLACE	PAULINE MELVILLE
DR GATTY	RODDY MAUDE-ROXBY
NURSE	FRANCESCA LONGRIGG
HOSPITAL DOCTOR	TANVEER GHANI
PHILLIS BLOKEY	JOANNA MAYS
LARRY FRISK	SEAN BEAN

EDITOR ALAN STRACHAN

ORIGINAL MUSIC BY DAVID DUNDAS AND RICK WENTWORTH

Photographed by Peter Hannan
Co-produced by Ray Cooper
Executive Producers George Harrison and
	Denis O'Brien
Produced by David Wimbury
Written and Directed by Bruce Robinson

Photographs by Sophie Baker